IF

Ironic Fundamentalism

A Journey from Anxiety to Enlightenment

by
Kirsty Lucinda Allan

Introduction from Morgana McCabe Allan, Ph.D

Published by Melissa English at

VICTORY INTERNATIONAL PRESS

Published by Melissa English,
Victory International Press.

ISBN: 978-1-913928-01-8

Cover design, diagrams and content layout by Jon Cheetham.
www.joncdesign.co.uk

Original cover art by Agsandrew.

Illustrations by Mark Lee Carter.

www.ironicfundamentalism.com

Dedicated to:

Victor and Gabriel

- my little heroes and
my biggest joy.

CONTENTS

ABOUT THE AUTHOR

Living in the 'avant-garden of life', Kirsty Lucinda Allan has led a curious career.

Born in 1982 in Scotland, Kirsty was raised in East Kilbride, near Glasgow. Attending local schools and ballet classes, she was a quiet, studious child, yet secretly she was fascinated by the 'big questions', the unconventional and the outré. Studying ancient mysticism, magick and comparative religion as soon as she could hold an encyclopedia, keeping snakes by age ten and practicing hypnosis by 12, she was perhaps always destined to become a 'maverick' in her fields.

In the 1990s, Kirsty was a child fashion model and junior ballerina for the Scottish Ballet Company, but her ambitions were curtailed by her developing body shape being deemed 'unsuitable' for either career. As an alternative thinker, these rejections laid the foundation for later adventures challenging body and beauty norms.

As an undergraduate psychology student at the University of Glasgow, Kirsty created *Ministry of Burlesque* as a project to help her and others overcome Anxiety surrounding body image. In doing so, she became an accidental arts movement leader and is considered one of the pioneers of the modern burlesque renaissance. As a 'student hobby that got out of hand', she has produced, directed and written approximately 1,000 shows, workshops and media projects celebrating body and beauty diversity.

In also landing (cat-like) in the world of corsetry, latex, fetish and alternative fashion, her subversive appeal led to many worldwide magazine covers (including prestigious art publication 125 magazine), international catwalks and art gallery exhibitions. With many still commenting on her Peter Pan-like youthfulness today, she says she 'keeps a special painting in the attic'.

Adding to her remarkable portfolio, Kirsty was also a formal paranormal investigator and became a consultant for mainstream television and leisure groups on matters of hauntings, vampires and psychic phenomena. By age 23 her first business cards read 'Pinup, Performer, Paranormal Investigator'.

As a postgraduate, Kirsty has studied at both the University of Edinburgh and University of Manchester acquiring further certificates in the fields of parapsychology and mental health interventions. She continues her personal study today - specialising in consciousness research, psycho-spirituality and transpersonal psychology.

Through her unusual career in both avant-garde arts and science, she has developed many unique wellbeing workshops and personal development courses inspired by the beauty and insight in everything she encounters.

Kirsty lives in an old (happily haunted) 17th Century home in the romantic Lake District, UK with her husband Jon, two children (Victor and Gabriel), two cats, two pythons and a tarantula. She continues to write, create and coach others to realise their potential through expansive consciousness.

FORWARD

We live in a world and time where there has been an explosion of anxiety among so many people. There are many reasons for the increase in anxiety that reflect the changes in our lives - especially in a new world of non-stop information and technological change.

We can't turn back the hands of time and retreat to a slower paced world, so we have to deal with the reality of anxiety. Yet for too many the only way of dealing with it is to resort to prescription medicine that masks the problem and doesn't solve or resolve it.

This book 'Ironic Fundamentalism' by Kirsty Lucinda Allan offers a unique and fresh approach to reframe the problem and turn what appears to be a weakness into a strength - a superpower.

See shares a "What If" approach that allows the reader (and the person with anxiety) to see anxiety with a different perspective and strategy - to use it as a tool to straighten themselves. Kirsty offers the reader a chance to transcend anxiety itself offering a potent approach that will empower you.

I encourage everyone with anxiety - or if you have a family member or friend who is suffering from it - to read this book and apply it to their lives.

John Duffy
Movie Producer and Public Speaker

ACKNOWLEDGEMENTS

After realising that the concept of Ironic Fundamentalism had been in my head for decades, it was time to get it out of there and available to others. I likely would have not gone beyond blogging and editing secret versions forever storing them on my MacBook until I saw the beautiful confidence that others had in both IF and in me as a writer. It is my lifetime's experience so far and I expect it is a milestone on my own hero(ine)'s journey of helping others to heal and grow.

I would like to personally thank my publisher Melissa at VIP International for keeping me accountable despite my own anxieties, for her unwavering faith and enthusiasm in the project. Morgana whom I call 'the headmistress of manifestation', for bringing about so much opportunity and nurturing to my life.

To my husband Jon for all the edits and diagrams, being my sounding board for the wackier ideas that came up and being an amazing father to our little children, especially when I had deadlines and doodles to make.

To movie producer John Duffy for seeing the value in taking bold steps and new directions both in my book as well as in the big movies of all our lives. To Mark Lee Carter who was able to take my random notions and turn them in to the adorable cartoons within.

To Emma, Diane and Diane, Keith, Kelly, Michael, Rachel, Dani, Heather-Anne, Robin and all who held space for me, listened, read and fed back when this book was either a collection of word salad or I feared it was 50,000 words of cobbleballs. To my parents, aunt and all those who have supported me over the years through my curious life decisions and career directions.

Thank you to all who have ever supported me and also those who have provoked Anxiety in me.

Thank you to all who take part and engage with IF.

Thank you to Anxiety itself, the unlikely teacher who has taught me the ironic key to personal illumination.

Kirsty Lucinda Allan

I would like to thank my parents Gray and Elaine Williams for always teaching me to follow my dreams and do the best work I could do. I would also like to thank my ex-husband, Jason English for showing me that anxiety is a very normal thing and nothing to be ashamed of.

I would finally like to thank Kirsty Lucinda Allan for prompting me to assist with this important project. You have changed my life more than you can ever know in such a short time!

Melissa English, VIP International
Publisher and Producer

INTRODUCTION

by Morgana McCabe Allan, Ph.D

In reading the manuscript for this book, I'm reminded just how big a problem anxiety is. Not only because it makes us turn home to double check the door is locked or keeps us from taking the leap into the great unknown of following our dreams, but because it is fundamentally collective in its nature. Anxiety is contagious.

That's almost certainly not blowing your mind right now. We all know we're anxious when our partners, or kids, or parents are anxious. But its bigger than that, because although it is an embodied emotion that transmits to the bodies around us, it's also cultural. We pick up patterns of anxiety from others, and we transmit them - sometimes on a massive scale. The better we learn to get a handle on it, the more we change the world around us for the better.

One of my favourite ways of discussing this with classes is the Reformation, because it's an example that's already played out, unlike something more contemporary and still ongoing. Before the Reformation the Western world was dominated by the Catholic Church, which preached a doctrine that provided all souls a 'way into Heaven' that looked a lot like this

- You die with a tally of sins on your soul.

- These amount to a certain time in purgatory (which is a hell), but after it you get into Heaven. You may be a VERY long time in there, but you will get out.

- There are LOTS of ways to reduce the time there by securing indulgences (essentially gift certificates to put towards your time of suffering). These included good works, pilgrimages and donating generously to the Church and having generations of your descendants pray your sins away for you for decades to come. For context, before the Reformation, indulgences could be worth hundreds of thousands of years in purgatory. People had a high degree of confidence in their eternal fate.

Yes, they were anxious about whether their crops would yield, their infants would survive, their husbands would play away, but fundamentally they were not anxious about what the longest-of-long term future held.

Until one day some people started to share new ideas. Ideas like indulgences are worth nothing, and worse - purgatory isn't even real. When you die you get weighed on your merit right then and there, and there is no do-over. In fact, if you even have those indulgences you're actually damned because they are not in the Bible. Oh also, there isn't a space for everyone in Heaven - only some people. They will be the best people. So you have to get it ALL right now, ok?

Those ideas made a lot of people anxious. Very, very anxious. Because nobody wants to go to hell. Peter Matheson highlights that this shift was characterised by a culture of intense anxiety over one's eternal fate. The witch trials were born. Witch trials were a lot like those lines of flares you see in medieval movies, where each bonfire is lit sequentially to pass a message across a kingdom. As soon as news of one witch trial flares a rash would follow, sometimes becoming a witch panic. Witch panics swept across European nations leaving death in their wake, and they are often very badly interpreted in scholarship and popular culture. They were not political plays. They were not money and land grabs. They were not 'the patriarchy.' Of course, a few cases were some of those things (or all of them). But the vast majority were ordinary people with nothing to gain, who were trapped in religious shame and deep anxiety about their eternal fate, and so terrified of agents of evil acting in their lives to threaten their place in Heaven that they accused their neighbours of witchcraft.

In Scotland and many other places, women accusing other women of similar status made up the majority of accusations, and the focus on what are essentially signs of culturally 'bad' motherhood. For example, let's say I'm a woman with a thin sick child and I'm not producing milk. That's culturally 'bad' motherhood. There's nothing I can do about it: there used to be magic, but of course consulting with a healer is now consulting with a witch; there used to be purgatory, but that's gone too. So I now have two choices - accept that I'm a bad mother and I'm going to hell OR accuse another woman with an uncommonly big, healthy baby of stealing my milk, my child or my husband, or cursing me.

As soon as that girl gets executed for witchcraft, even before then, a LOT of people start feeling very anxious... is that a spell they're feeling on them? It looks like a spell...Yep, definitely feeling that spell, and maybe it's not an old spell...Did she have a coven around here?

And then there is the other side of this anxiety-fest "Am I the next victim of this witch hunt?".

This may seem very far away from today, but as Kirsty so eloquently highlights throughout the book, we are all prone to this kind of thinking - what if I am next? Is there more bad stuff coming? Could it be dangerous to share this with people? Will people accept me? And the pattern is one of many with much deeper cultural roots than we realise. We think we are alone in our anxieties, but in truth we are all very much there together, assuming everyone else might be the witch or maybe think we are the witch, and maybe we better just go home actually. Phew.

Every time we take part in this pattern we are also perpetuating it. There may no longer be witch hunts, but it's important to remember that the witch hunts were just one cultural expression of the exact same fears and beliefs that still underpin many of our anxieties today, in evolutionary terms those days were... well... earlier today.

Let's take one example: anxiety about not getting it right first try.

Parents with this anxiety don't model healthy risk taking to their children, because they are averse to it themselves. They don't speak in language that opens up to the possibility that with great risk comes great reward. They may pay lip service to the idea that "you can be anything you want, honey" but they don't actually model aspiring to create, do, or be more. Their kids don't see them try, fail, and try again. They participate in social structures that train their children to get it right first try or fail - the entire concept of the examination is founded on this. Those children go onto further education where they don't push the envelope in their field, they don't even get close.

Firstly, they have no practice of it, their eye is not trained to see potential, nor their mind to think in possibility. Secondly, they are conditioned to be rewarded for getting it right and there is an extremely high possibility when out on the edge of anything (in fact, I can almost certainly guarantee it) that some people will NOT like what you do and there will be more 'wrong' than right. There are a lot of dead ends on the way to pretty much anywhere that nobody has gone before. Thirdly, even if they DO all of that, and they get to that greatness, there is even more anxiety waiting because we are taught to conform so effectively that many people don't share great work in fear of rejection as a fake or failure. Work that might change the world, and goes unseen into the rotting carcass of knowledge known as 'the grey literature' of unpublished works. Cause of death: imposter syndrome.

Imposter syndrome is perhaps the anxiety I can speak the most personally to, though definitely not the only one. I remember as a fresh-faced postgraduate asking the head of my department "Jeremy, when will this terrible feeling end. When do you stop feeling like an imposter and start feeling ok again?" His reply was not encouraging. For brevity and the wellbeing of all, I will paraphrase as "Oh Morgana, that's not how it works, it gets bigger and bigger." He was right, but he was also wrong. Mine has (and continues) to get bigger and bigger. But as Kirsty will guide you, I learned to engage it not as a burden I must carry, but as the wind at my back. Imposter syndrome about my research drove me to make it better, and to have conversations with incredible specialists that elevated everything I created. Because of it (not in spite of it) I went to as many conferences as I could, to get as much peer feedback as possible on as many areas as possible, of my studies in quantum anthropology. By ditching the 'positive' and 'negative' in feedback, and seeing it all as feedback, my work grew so much stronger, and at the same time I built a body of evidence that I was not an imposter. At least for today. Every day is a new day - that particular anxiety always comes back - and so the trick I've learned is to expect it. Each time it's bigger, but I'm bigger too: I'm learning with it, through it, even as it.

Anxiety is contagious, and it's cost is far higher that we might ever think as we put off writing our books, creating our course, telling our stories, performing our truth and all of these other important, anxiety inducing things in order to focus on something more tangible and present - like making sure the house is perfect in case the neighbours stop by unannounced for example. There's nothing like procrastinating on something that makes you too anxious to start, by working on something else that makes you anxious, after all.

What really speaks to me about Kirsty's work is that by encouraging us to see anxiety as normal, it allows for new possibilities. Instead of something to be cured (it goes all the way back to the first mammals in brain terms, so that's a tall order) it's something to be befriended. A true quantum psychologist, her view is refreshing: that the exact thing which has been keeping us all small could be the same thing that propels us to new heights of consciousness, if we learn to understand it better.

The beauty of this is that in working on ourselves we are actually serving the collective. As we change the conversation we have within, the language we use and the behaviours we model begin to shift. Enough people shifting creates an unstoppable ripple because, as Kirsty walks us through, anxiety responds to evidence. Enough evidence is all cultural change is waiting for. And those witch trials? They ended when the judicial system changed to put the burden of proof on the prosecution.

It was hard to prove witches guilty, which mean fewer were executed. With fewer executed, there was less anxiety in the air about whether witchcraft was afoot, which meant fewer accusations. Fewer accusations has to mean fewer witches, right? Anxiety about witches fades, until witches are just a quiet echo, inspiration for creative bedtime stories for children, empowerment for women seeking to reclaim their wild hearts, where they were once as present and dangerous amongst us as any contemporary threat could ever be.

Our personal anxieties, fears and phobias, lovingly treated, can likewise become sources of inspiration and empowerment. Kirsty is a wonderful guide on this journey offering both professional and personal experience. As we follow her through the dark spaces of anxiety there is light to be found - for example in recognising that experiences and decisions themselves as not 'right or wrong', but for the meaning we choose to make for them.

What If...?

An anxious mind is a living mind.

It is not only a brain that thinks (and overthinks) upon the big questions of Life, The Universe and Everything, it is also the echoing voice of a heart that truly cares. Learning to listen to those inner experiences we call 'Anxiety' can give us clarity and guide us to grow beyond the illusory limitations of fear, illness and exhaustion - and instead choose growth, health and creativity.

What if Anxiety is the training ground for extraordinary thinking and feeling?

What if we can direct our anxious experiences in a new direction and turn fear into growth?

What if as an anxious person you have been training your whole life to be an amazing manifestor?

WHAT is the book about?

Choice.

This is a book about asking 'What If...' and learning to choose what you want in life, rather than what you fear.

It is also a book based on my own direct experiences of Anxiety and the empowering lessons I have learned. I have been my own 'guinea pig' in life as I have experimented and adventured, tried and tested.

This is a book about the surprising and thoroughly ironic relationship between Anxiety and personal Enlightenment. This book is designed to guide those who experience Anxiety, not to simply 'cope' and 'manage their symptoms', but instead to *transcend* them.

Curious? I hope so.

Your living mind can be also likened to an active temple, school or gym and if you show up for service, lessons or training, you'll come to see how that once overbearing teacher named Anxiety might just be your personal inner guru. If you pay attention, you will learn secrets hidden within yourself, come to see the interconnected beauty of all things and have the faith to step forward and act as the leading player in your own life story.

This book is not intended as therapy or a substitute for clinical intervention, instead, it is intended as a companion for those seeking new perspectives and a mindset of personal growth. It is my sincere wish that these pages will help others to accept themselves fully (Anxiety and all!) instead of battling an imaginary war with the self and to give themselves permission to trust in curiosity, forge their path and do extraordinary things.

What if Reality is what we make it?

What if... the nature of life, the universe and everything is fundamentally *paradoxical* (and therefore, so is everything you experience)?

With this in mind...

What if... as an anxious person, you are actually in possession of powerful mental, physical and emotional skills?

What if... by embracing this *personal paradox*, you can transmute self-doubt into self-belief? Illness into health? Exhaustion into creativity?

What if... by further embracing the bigger *united paradox of all things*, you can use your skills to transcend Anxiety toward your own personal Enlightenment?

You can.

I call this the practical theory of *Ironic Fundamentalism*. Catchy, right?

Instead of resenting, resisting or fearing your experience of Anxiety *what if* you could use it for your own good, by finding the ironic wisdom it teaches you?

What would you do with this newly found freedom? What extra energy would you have to direct? What potential would you unleash? What adventures would you go on? What would you *create*?

Why IF?

Whether we are diagnosed by a professional or self-diagnose with 'Anxiety', we have choices.

We can do nothing, or we can do something - or even many things. We can intervene in any problems. We can talk with others, pick up self-help books and visit websites, try alternative or complementary practitioners, healers and 'natural' remedies. There are various forms of holistic, spiritual and psychological therapy and, where it is a condition of *disordered* worry, we can also go to the medical and clinical world for advice and medication - if we choose to.

It's all about *choices* *.

* *As you are reading (or perhaps listening to) this sentence, you have obviously made a choice to explore beyond your experience of Anxiety. You have actually done so much more than you probably realise already - so give yourself a fiver to spend on something nice, just for you. Being kind to yourself is super important in self-care. In fact, make it a tenner.*

Any one of these interventions or a combination might be great for one person and yet do sod all for another. This is simply because Anxiety is a personal multi-faceted experience and is therefore unique to the individual. There is no 'cure' and there doesn't need to be one. Some techniques or interventions can knock out some of the '*symptoms*' (or sensations as I prefer to call them) for some people, and although this can bring huge relief it may not address the underlying root cause of the overall experience. Similarly, in many therapy styles, we typically learn to identify and *manage* our thoughts and feelings through mental techniques, but do we ever really move on from them?

Anxiety is made up of problematic or painful *physical symptoms*, unhelpful *behaviour* or habits, negative *thoughts*, and upsetting *feelings*. Right?

Consider right away, that with such adjectives in place the whole experience is set up to be viewed unequivocally as *bad* and *detrimental*. We often regard the 'manifestation' of Anxiety as we would a poltergeist in a horror movie; that it is the ghostly echo of some personal (metaphorical of course) restless demon - but the reality is that we are not 'possessed' by anything other than our own self-limiting beliefs.

If we think bigger than the Anxiety experience itself, we see that we are *more than it.* We are bigger than it. We are the ones having the experience; therefore we must be hosting it. It is not happening 'to us' as though we are subject to an external tormenting force, but instead it is happening *within* us - or even 'through us' when we begin to work *with it.* As Eckhart Tolle (author of the wonderful book *The Power of Now*) so eloquently says "You are not your thoughts".

We are more than our thoughts, our feelings, and our habits. We are more than all our experiences put together. We are so much more than the sum of our problems. There are many more dimensions to our human experience, that go unaddressed by the usual prescribed remedies and strategies. As Czech psychiatrist and one of the founding fathers of transpersonal psychology observed:

> *"The psyche of the individual is commensurate*
> *with the totality of creative energy. This requires a most*
> *radical revision of Western psychology."*
> **Stanislav Grof**

Where many people remain in a state of 'managing' their Anxiety, often for life, their identities also remain stuck; attached to Anxiety as a label defining some limiting aspect of themselves. They proceed in life by orienting their decisions around it as though tethered to a Wizard of Oz style phantom controller who may or may not give permission for any kind of personal progress.

It's that old "Oh, I have Anxiety..." narrative that people repeat to themselves and others to justify, explain and avoid things, but the irony here is that no one 'has' Anxiety - we *experience* it. We actually create it too. So, why stop at just 'managing your symptoms'?

Think again about the idea of 'managing' or 'coping'... Is this it? Is this the ultimate and best way forward?

Do you really just want to 'cope'? Sure, you may be coping better with some of the 'symptoms' but ironically, is this practice of coping actually maintaining a mindset that orbits your entire being *around* Anxiety as a problem?

> *"Use your fear... it can take you to the place*
> *where you store your courage."*
> **Amelia Earhardt**

Would you prefer to evolve from it instead?

You see, I believe that with a tiny bit of faith and a fistful of derring-do we can go beyond Anxiety 'management'. Rather than fight with it, flee or hide from it we can tame its restless energy, saddle up and ride into the proverbial light on a personal journey. We can go beyond 'coping' and grow toward ataraxia - a lovely poetic word for a 'state of serenity'.

Why did I write this?

I consider myself lucky because I have first-hand lived experience of disordered, disabling, out-of-control Anxiety. Yep, LUCKY. This is because I have found the ironic power it holds, and I have come to see it as my internal 'guru'.

A difficult cantankerous old git of a guru at times, perhaps, but none the less a teacher of truth through honest personal (and sometimes painful) reflection.

I have experienced Anxiety in many forms for as long as I can remember and yet, in spite of all the self-doubt I keep finding myself on adventures.

I'm very curious by nature and so I make a point of exploring the 'avant-garden' of life. On a journey of personal growth, I have travelled many unusual paths, even forging new ones at times - new paths that others would come to follow soon after.

This book is one of the most exciting adventures yet because it feels so risky to be personally open and also... to be open to criticism. Ironically, it was in recognising this worry I knew that IF needed to be out of my head and available to yours because maybe, you might take encouragement to share your ideas too.

Why the capitalisation of Anxiety?

Creative choice. I feel it gives the experience of Anxiety a name. A sense of 'being' as though it has a personality. I like to anthropomorphise (put human qualities on to non-human things), like when muddy boots abandoned in a hallway look 'sleepy', or when cats walk like they are in a fashion show or when I tell my toddlers that the bin is hungry for their rubbish or when doodling some mice playing trumpets - that sort of thing.

In a therapeutic sense, metaphors and anthropomorphism help create an easy flowing sense of concept engagement, especially where it can be fraught with difficult emotions.

Same Old Story Brand New Script

From ancient wisdom to modern spirituality, our true nature as 'beings' does not have to remain a Hermetically sealed mystery.

Whether historical or mythical, the journey of enlightenment generally follows the same path - ubiquitously known today as 'the hero's journey' after the work of mythology expert Joseph Campbell and his influential work, *Hero with a Thousand Faces*. 'The hero's journey' is widely regarded as an archetypal narrative, a kind of template for storytelling across our favourite books and movies. From the ancient classics to Tolkien's beautifully crafted fae adventurers, the intergalactic excitement of Star Wars and the young heroes and heroines of the Harry Potter series, this journey is seen time and time again inspiring and enthralling its fans as each story shows the hero(ine)* being called to action, leaving home for a journey of ultimate self-discovery fraught with moral turmoil, challenges and doubt, eventually to return home to the benefit of their people - but is in themselves, changed forever.

*FYI, I'll continue using the term 'hero' as an all-encompassing non-gender specific noun.

So too is this story detailed in the 22 'points' of self-discovery as mapped on the major arcana of tarot cards. The journey goes from The Fool (an innocent person who becomes the hero) who steps forward on an adventure like a child (unbiased and yet also unprepared) going through the deck experiencing the key points of wisdom and self-discovery, until finally arriving at The World symbolising personal fulfilment.

From the starvation of the Buddha to the crucifixion of Jesus and to the exile of the Dalai Lama, our great sages, gurus and spiritual teachers all experienced great suffering in one monumental way or another - before 'attaining enlightenment' and leaving a legacy that would lead others along their 'path', their 'way' or in their 'light'.

We all suffer in different ways, at different 'points' in life. Anxiety is certainly one way. Most people are trained to perceive these points as negative - to be avoided, boxed up, repressed, and even lamented. But what IF there was paradoxical truth? That as these spiritual histories, biographies, myths and stories all tell us, that through suffering there is ultimate peace? That suffering and peace are two sides of the same thing, co-existing and determined by one another? It is what you do with the suffering - as an experience - that makes the difference between sagacity and sadness.

Considering the literary metaphor further where our hero's journey may be fraught with challenges - these could be our life chapter markers. Where one chapter of a story ends and it becomes the beginning of a new one, we often feel we are on a 'cliff hanger' or 'edge' or that there is some form of change afoot - or, we take a pause for rest and reflection. Often, in this metaphorical literary gap between life chapters, we feel excited or *anxious* about what will come next. You see, excitement and Anxiety are also two sides of a same coin. There are many double-sided coins in your hero's purse and whether you see them as small change or gold is actually up to you. Wealth is an energy, perceived and transmuted - not a commodity.

"The cave you fear to enter holds the treasure you seek."
Joseph Campbell

With Ironic Fundamentalism, I see personal wellbeing struggles as just such key opportunities for insight. For example, going to the gym can hurt your muscles like hell but you learn just how strong you are - and you can become excited about your growth, even learn to enjoy the sensation of painful muscles. Experiencing Anxiety does not need to be an illness or unfortunate trait affecting you, keeping you back, preventing you doing things - it can instead be a spiritual gym in which you grow stronger. It can be an internal compass guiding you on a journey of self-actualisation.

You too can choose this. This is your call to action. You are the hero(ine).

Not a Map...

This book is not a map - because quite simply your journey has no map as you have yet to tread the ground. Ironically, it may well be in this precise uncertainty of 'where am I going?' that your personal angst has taken root. Instead, think of this book as a companion who reminds you to look within as well as ahead, to look up to the stars at night when you feel you are in the dark and to navigate beyond any obstacles in your path, so you can forge your own road ahead.

A Picture Paints a Thousand Words

There are a lot of metaphors, similes and attempted aphorisms in this book. I love wordplay as it is like painting with words and after all, 'a picture paints a thousand words' or so I've heard. The theory and practice of what I have called 'Ironic Fundamentalism' involves a thoughtful and feeling-based approach and so to present slippery ideas in a more 'grasp-able' useful way there are diagrams by my husband Jon and cartoons too (my thoughts illustrated by the wonderful Mark Carter).

I hope that as well as being a ponder upon the nature of being, this book will also provide a practical gem or two that you can conjure to mind any time and use as your mantras. You see, I have learned that where Anxiety itself is feared, shunned, and shamed - it could instead be embraced, accepted, and even loved... and when we love, we grow...

CHAPTER ONE

ANXIETY - IT'S NOTHING TO WORRY ABOUT

WHAT is Anxiety?

Put simply, Anxiety is an intolerance to *uncertainty*. Just like when the body is intolerant to lactose or wheat it goes to extravagant lengths to 'eject' the offending perceived toxin (in erm, one way or another) as though it is under attack. Similarly, Anxiety is a natural but often misfiring defence mechanism. When anxious, we are unable to accept and digest the unpredictable changing nature of reality before us. This can leave us feeling that we might expire any moment.

Anxiety is that overprotective nan who wants to keep you in a bubble of sweaty blankets whilst stroking your cheek with unnerving words of 'there, there, stay nice and safe, here with nan-nan...' rather than let you go play. It is that drunk best friend who means well by grabbing your phone and texting your ex whilst you are in the loo. It is trying to keep you safe but ironically it makes you ill.

When going full throttle, Anxiety leads to Panic (which is the physical body's 'fight or flight process'). Your fight or flight response is a flood of adrenaline caused by your somewhat ironically named 'sympathetic nervous system'. This system is trying to save you from all sorts of imagined and unseen forces -

but in doing so, it gives a sterling impression that it is trying to kill you. It tries to save you from danger but creates what feels like Armageddon on your nerves.

Typical situations where Anxiety occurs include...

- Thinking about the past
- Thinking about the future
- Busy places, crowds, queues
- Transport and Travel
- Meeting new people
- Exams and tests
- Medical and health appointments
- Family and social gatherings
- Public speaking or performance
- Gym, swimming pool, changing room
- School, workplace
- Performance reviews, criticism
- Opening mail (including email)
- Trying new medicines or treatments
- New job or course
- Preparing food
- Eating in front of others
- Social Media
- Writing email and making phone calls
- Voting
- Looking in mirrors

- Watching the news or reading newspapers
- Watching horror films (sometimes I wonder that the news should be rated as such)
- Seeing blood
- Seeing spiders, snakes, etc.
- Looking at and adding to 'To Do' lists...

Can you add to this list? I bet you 10p that you can.

Typical Symptoms

I have often been frustrated by those who make unhelpful comments like 'oh, anxiety? That's just all in your head'. Now I am absolutely not a medical doctor, however, I'm pretty sure the head is part of the body and quite an important one too. Don't ever let anyone rubbish or diminish your very real 100%-happening-in-the-physical-world experience. Politely suggest that they go get their head checked.

When Anxiety occurs (and our fight or flight response is activated), we get a load of unpleasant things going on in the body - they can be frightening too as they are often debilitating and some (e.g. tight chest, pain, sweating) are similar to the signs of particularly worrying things like heart attacks.

The sensations of Anxiety and especially in the more sudden and severe form of panic, can actually be readily explained though as your body is preparing to fight, flee (or freeze/hide). Your heart is working really hard to get you ready for action and your blood is pumping faster and - it is moving away from your extremities into the big muscles and toward your major organs. You are breathing faster and taking in more oxygen than is comfortable (hyperventilating). Your glands are also releasing stress hormones to heighten your senses to help you locate danger quickly. Your digestive system is erm, well trying to 'lighten the load' and expel any potential toxins.

The body has a wisdom of its own. It evaluates and regulates its interaction with the world. From acts that we often do not notice e.g. fighting disease and regulating temperature to those unexpected acts we cannot fail to notice and then over-interpret like the following list...

Your experience might involve:

- Racing thoughts
- Heart pounding
- Sweating
- Headaches
- Dizziness
- Nausea
- Sudden bowl movements
- Bladder urgency
- Heightened senses (everything is LOUD and/or 'too bright')
- Dry mouth or thirst
- Tight or painful chest
- Cold or clammy hands
- Sleep disturbances
- Jelly legs...

Can you add to this list? I bet you 10p *and* a biscuit that you can.

Interestingly, these are all possibly present in the general feeling of excitement. What makes it unpleasant in many ways is the context in which we have the experience, and the 'source' or trigger is unlikely to be something we want. Imagine you are told you've won the lottery - what feelings do you start to notice? Butterflies in the tummy? Racing thoughts?

What IF, instead of 'physical symptoms' we simply notice our physical *experience*? Thus, we do away with the loaded sentiment of 'symptoms' - which are never constructive or enabling, only negative, painful and disabling. For the sake of familiarity and consistency, I will refer to 'symptoms' as we progress though!

But really... why stick to the madness of labelling our experience as automatically negative? Why not rename that shaky nausea, the jelly legs, the sweats, the racing heart and pounding head to be excitement rather than Anxiety? They are after all, the same thing or set of things - differing only by name according to interpretation.

It's worth considering that language colours everything, for example; the word 'crisis' also means opportunity in Chinese. 'Emergency' actually means 'emergence' where for example, in Shamanic cultures a mental health crisis is seen as a spiritual transformation - an emergence of something new from old, a process of evolving. Not necessarily a bad thing.

To take it further, the concept of 'nominative determinism' suggests that as we inherit or 'take on' names, we act them out - as though they predict our futures. Whether the name is bestowed at birth or assumed. I once knew someone called Matt Black who became a painter and decorator. My friend Morgana became an accidental expert in early modern witchcraft and fairy beliefs through her academic studies of how our reality and identity emerge from and co-create the webwork of connections with materials, people, places and things that we engage with. Think about performers choosing their own stage names; in my many years of experience, I could very often kind of predict a performer's career path according to their name. As though destiny is literally written in our names. Thinking Biblically, the 'Word' is the beginning of all things and, as Adam names the animals we took a sense of power over those animals - those things we (Adam) named. In other ancient mystical traditions, secret magical names are assumed by the individual and kept entirely private - for exactly this reason, to keep the power with the *namer* and not the *named*.

Choose the context of your language to work for you - not against you. This goes for the names you call yourself. Inner critic or otherwise.

Think back to times when you were excited and notice what you experienced. Maybe it was going on a roller-coaster, buying your first car, walking up the aisle on your wedding day or meeting your grandchild for the first time. What comes to mind?

Furthermore, a short sudden burst of exercise will bring about these symptoms too. Ironically, you can actually help mitigate the symptoms if you DO go for a quick run - the energy that's suddenly released into and through your body and mind is overwhelming because it isn't being used, it doesn't have anywhere to go. Exercise (including healthy sex) is one of the absolute best things you can do for your self-care as it helps to balance your energy systems and helps you grow.

Since the word 'symptoms' is medically loaded - it carries automatic negative associations of illness, let's call them 'physical sensations' from here on.

Typical Thoughts

When we experience Anxiety we fail to notice that our thoughts are not the shining moments of sense or reason that we assume. We often take something as being automatically true because it 'fits' our theories or assumptions. We ignore evidence to the contrary and even lend credibility to falsehoods because they 'could be' true. The irony here is that we are choosing to do so. Furthermore, we don't even realise we have a choice because we are already too busy buying in to another false assumption - namely, 'that we don't have a choice'. Feel free to scratch your head here. Notice that it probably became itchy because of the suggestion you might want to scratch it. It wasn't itchy before, right? Caveat Emptor - buyer beware! Don't buy into an idea just because it's there.

So, I suggested *something* and you had a real physiological response to it. Anxiety is the same. You think a worry and bam! You're feeling it in your body as tension, nausea, pain, shakiness, etc. The thought has become *embodied*. You have created the proverbial itch. Or maybe I did, it doesn't really matter who said what... what matters is that you notice the symbiotic link between thinking and feeling.

Some typical thoughts run along the lines of:

- What if they don't like me?
- What if I said the wrong thing?
- Is my headache a sign of a tumour?
- Is that lump more than just suspicious?
- What will happen if I can't pay my bills?

- Is it possible that I'm to blame for...?
- What if there's an accident?
- How will I manage if she leaves?
- What will happen to my dog if...?
- What if Hell is real?
- What if I'm a 'bad person'?
- What if it is all my fault?

Can you add to this list? I bet you 10p *and* a biscuit and one of those nice coconut things that you can.

One of my favourite aspects of psyche-stuff to examine with others is their thinking habits. I get excited about what is known as the 'cognitive distortions' or 'thinking errors', based on the work of psychiatrist Aaron Beck in the 1960s. The insightful legacy of Beck's work and wisdom is widely utilised in therapeutic practice today, especially with the popular and successful approach of *Cognitive Behavioural Therapy* (CBT). Here are the distortions (in no particular order). Have fun identifying yourself, your husband, your boss and maybe even your dog...

The Cognitive Distortions

1. All or Nothing (black or white, polarised or dichotomous) thinking

Error is in thinking there is 1 or 0, this or that, rather than a continuum between two points.

E.g. "If Sandra doesn't get my spatula joke then I'm entirely unfunny to all beings."

E.g. "If Barry gets this part in the play then I'll never get ahead in my own career."

2. Catastrophising

Error is in assuming that a possible negative prediction of the future is somehow a certainty, especially in dismissing all other less dramatic outcomes and in particular dismissing or outright ignoring any positive outcomes.

E.g. "Oh my various gods! We are all gonna die of heart attacks because I can't cook nice things."

E.g. "If Gary gets that promotion, this company is doomed and we are all out of work."

3. Emotional Reasoning

Error occurs because you 'feel' something to be true so strongly, despite all evidence against it.

E.g. "I'm a rubbish dad (because I really feel useless when playing dollies)."

E.g. "I feel really anxious because that snake is definitely scared and going to bite me."

E.g. "I feel offended by that comment so those people must be in the wrong."

4. Labelling

The annoying habit of bias assumption, labelling yourself or others according to stereotypes and personal heuristics.

E.g. "Ughh, that guy hates me because he's a prime example of toxic masculinity/patriarchy/..."

E.g. "Look at her posh clothes, she won't be willing to share her table with the likes of me."

5. Magnification/Minimisation

The error of magnifying any potential problem or deficit whilst also minimising any benefit or opportunity. *Also, disqualifying* any positive experiences, facts or evidence as though they do NOT count.

E.g. "If I don't get an A++ on this one test I will be a failure and even though I have 50 years experience and training and invented the thing in question - it's just not as relevant."

E.g. "That time I solved world hunger, rescued the village children and then saved the universe from exploding? Oh well, that was just me looking for attention I suppose."

E.g. "Even though he flew to the moon and back to ask me out on a date, I just know he doesn't fancy me."

6. Mental Filter (or 'selective abstraction')

The error of paying attention to one negative idea or comment other than whole situation.

E.g. "I was advised to enhance my customer communication skills so despite the fact that in all other aspects of my work I had really positive feedback, I'm poop at my job."

E.g. "That one bad review of my screenplay where the critic said I was 'trite' means that all the 90,000 good reviews are wrong."

7. Mind Reading

The error of assuming you know what someone else is thinking/ feeling or, what motivates their thoughts and feelings.

E.g. "I bet she expects me to fail - she has never had any faith in my work."

E.g. "They don't want me here because they fear my mind-reading abilities."

E.g. "When Phyllis said she liked my shoes, she was probably just being nice because she thinks my socks suck. I have sucky socks."

8. Overgeneralisation or 'global thinking'

The error is where you make sweeping conclusions - especially when they go way beyond the situation in mind.

E.g. "That Susan girl I met online was nothing like she appeared in real life - so I don't trust women."

E.g. "Because no one has hired me for this so far, it means I'm totally unemployable."

E.g. "My parents' generation are from a different era, they don't understand modern technology."

9. Personalisation

The error is in thinking that something is occurring *because* of you rather than for other more likely reasons.

E.g. "The doctor was curt with me because I am annoying him with my complaints."

E.g. "I didn't get the opportunity because I'm unlucky."

10. Should/Must/Ought to statements (aka "imperatives")

The error is where you assume how yourself and others 'should' think, feel or behave. When projected onto others this extends to moralising which leads to a judgemental mindset - and judgemental mindsets keep us anchored in fear and suspicion.

E.g. "I SHOULD be earning enough to buy my parents a holiday home."

E.g. "Stuart really ought not to vote for that party if he wants..."

E.g. "They ought not to be proud of themselves about their campaign... they ought to feel embarrassed..."

Notice how often 'if' comes up and see *if* you can suggest alternative 'ifs' in each example. See how many of these habits are familiar to your mind and others.

Anxiety 'sufferers' could easily describe their experience as being in 'a dark place of doubt', and yet darkness is the best vantage point to see the light - and truly know it is there and not just hope it's there. It is in this dark dwelling place of *doubt* that *faith* is promoted. Ironic, right?

So here goes, here is the first fundamentally ironic truth to ponder.

What IF... Anxiety: it's nothing to worry about!?

When we worry, we doubt things - things we actually must have at least some faith in. You can only doubt a thing if you first hold some belief in it. If you can firstly realise that you are immersed in the darkness of doubt, then there is potential to see the light.

You see?

Let's elucidate further. Doubt and faith are differing natures of the same thing. You cannot have faith unless you have doubt and vice versa. Two sides of the same coin, opposite ends of the same spectrum - they are one, working together. It is in a conceptual convention of language that we create opposites. Anxiety is a range of experiences (mental, emotional, and physical symptoms) that occur when this doubt/faith spectrum is in flux. When we place our faith in something or someone, it's because we trust or believe in them enough to take a kind of hypothetical *risk*. It is the *risk* that creates opportunity for Anxiety to emerge.

Think back to the statement 'Anxiety is an intolerance to uncertainty'.

What if... Uncertainty is your key to freedom?

We fear we have no (or too little) control over bad things that *might* occur. However, when we are anxious we are leaning toward (or even fully immersed in) a strange sense of *certainty* of some impending calamity. Ironic, right? We 'manage' our fear of uncertainty by adopting a negative belief of certainty. No wonder Anxiety is exhausting!

What if the further irony here is that *uncertainty* is actually our way out of the anxious labyrinth? The uncertain nature of all things gives us far more room for hope - for neutral and positive outcomes. The neutral and the good potential outweighing the bad.

To do this we need to release our grip on the illusion of certainty and surrender to the uncertain nature of reality. It's not as terrifying as it first seems, this is an act of faith in yourself and in your reality. Besides, control is an illusion - there are always infinite factors at influence in any situation such as circumstance, happenstance, which day it is, what way the wind is blowing...

Think of something that spikes anxious thoughts and feelings in you and ask yourself...

Which is more likely: the exact specific thing(s) or outcomes you are worrying about right now or, something else from ALL the other possibilities?

(if the unknown 'something else' is worrying you, imagine it to be something beautiful like an unexpected gift, because this at least is just as likely!)

Which is preferable: holding on to the minimal amount of danger that might occur (the worst-case scenarios) or, instead allowing the maximum amount of all other potential to happen including unimagined awesomeness?

Which will you choose?

We also need Anxiety to be able to appreciate its opposite, ataraxia.

Anxiety is a state of distress, worry, suffering. By contrast, *ataraxia* is the state of 'freedom from Anxiety' (a state of calm, serenity, peace, tranquillity). However, for Ataraxia to have any *meaning* to us, we must first experience its opposite, Anxiety. Two sides of the same coin, two ends of the same spectrum. Two perspectives of the same events.

> *"Nothing in life is to be feared, it is only to be understood.*
> *Now is the time to understand more, so that we may fear less."*
> **Marie Curie**

The list of ironies is as endless as the stars, but you will discover that for yourself as you begin to see the *Ironic Fundamentalism* that is Life, The Universe and Everything.

So, 'Anxiety: it's nothing to worry about'? I am hoping this statement is a little provocative. Perhaps you find it funny? Or flippant and irritating? Perhaps you see a double pun (emphasis on the word 'nothing'?) or perhaps you have a sense of impending insight? Look for the irony.

Well, let me outline the fundamental irony of this statement - and it is twofold:

1. If you are an Anxiety sufferer, you probably 'worry about everything'. Well, *everything* in its totality encompasses well, everything, and so it cannot be specifically *any*-thing (because it is *every*-thing). So, everything is nothing specific.

   Hence, worrying about everything = worrying about nothing (specific).

2. Of course, there is also the further extension of the idea. Anxiety leads us to worry *not* about what is happening right *now* in the real world, instead it leads us to worry about hypothetical futures that do not exist and probably never will. These imagined futures are literally *nothing* beyond our anxious conjuring and, can appear and disappear with each pendulum swing of a ticking clock and firing neuron.

Yet, it is these *imagined* scenarios, these *nothings* that we fixate on.

Keep these key points in mind:

- Anxiety is an intolerance to uncertainty.
- Nothing is certain. Certainty is an unhelpful illusion of control.
- Surrendering to uncertainty dissolves the need for certainty.

Travelling a little further along the thought train, consider that our stars and planets exist in mostly 'empty space'. They are the things suspended in a kind of 'nothingness'. So too, within our bodies all our atoms are mostly 'empty space' with collections of busy little particles whizzing around in there doing what they do, having a marvellous time.

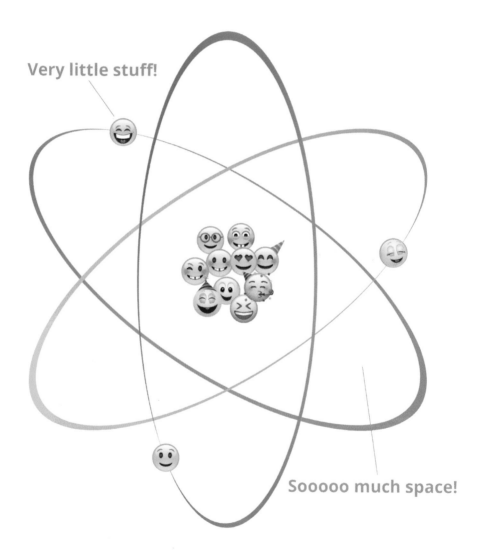

Very little stuff!

Sooooo much space!

So, the majority of anything is well, nothing. Everything and nothing are a paradoxical concept because everything exists within the nothing, has come from nothing, will return to nothing. We cannot be aware of experiencing one without the possibility of the other. We need each, for the other to exist. In a way, different things are just different arrangements of empty space and busy bits.

We will return to this idea in more detail later and what's more, it will become the foundation of your amazing practice and personal growth. After all, we need space to grow, right? Realising just how much of it we already have in us and around us, allows us to realise (and then actualise) the enormous potential we hold.

How awesome is this? It's atomic, it's cosmic scale awesome! It's YOU!

What IF... your own big butt is in the way?

There is a habit of assuming cause and effect in a *negative* direction. You realise of course, that you are choosing this direction, yes? You could choose a positive direction instead. The word 'but' then often follows. Notice how it butts in there to justify the negativity as in "Yes, I see that I'm being negative **but**...".

If your inner critic or someone else is parking their big butt on your ideas and stopping the flow of potentially very creative thoughts, hoof them off. Try this technique from Tudor Rickards' book *Creativity and Problem Solving at Work*:

Instead of '*Yes but...*' install a different line of '*Yes **and**...*'

This 'Yes and...' technique provokes creative thinking and I think it also helps to promote a sense of acceptance that the negative thought is there (remember we don't want to fight with it) *and* it also promotes expansive thinking. Creative thinking is at the heart if problem solving, novel and alternative ideas. The 'and' suggests that you can move on from the statement in any direction you choose rather than justifying it and holding onto it as though it has any truth.

E.g. "Yes, I see that I'm being negative **but**... It really feels true to me/my experience tells me..."

Replace with:

"Yes, I see that I'm being negative **and**... I can see that I can move forward too/my knowledge of Anxiety tells me it's not a fact."

It's time to move that but(t) and get out of your own way.

"Stop it, and give yourself a chance."
Aaron T. Beck

When I was studying for a post-graduate certificate in mental health interventions, we were told the story of the 'Two Wolves'. I've heard that it is a Native American parable but as I can't find an 'original source' to quote from, I'll creatively paraphrase it here (and where it originates from isn't really important - it is beautifully simple). It's all about choice.

'An elder speaks to a curious child to explain:

"There are two wolves that fight for control within every person. One wolf represents fear, lack and sadness, and the other represents joy, abundance and growth."

The child asks: "But which one will win?!"

The elder says: "The one you feed".'

Which one will you feed? Or if you are determined to feed both... which one gets the nice biscuits?

Worried about being 'needy'? No Need! Needs must...

At this juncture it makes sense to look at what our needs actually are - and how to identify them.

One of the simplest and most comprehensive ways to look at our needs is through psychologist Abraham Maslow's 'hierarchy of needs'. This shows a pyramid-like structure demonstrating 5 layers of needs. The foundation is the widest layer, supporting all others and is comprised of the basic Physiological needs (food, water, rest/sleep, shelter, warmth).

These needs must be fulfilled before a person can successfully ascend to fulfil the next layer which is Safety oriented (health, security, protection from accidents etc), then Social belonging (family, friendships, intimacy), Self-esteem (significance, being valuable to others and so on), all the way to the top of the pyramid where Self-actualisation is the goal.

Self-actualisation is considered to be the fulfilment of one's personal potential in this case, but many including Maslow have posited that there are further opportunities to ascend, for example in terms of transcendence and spirituality where we align with our big, universal or spiritual values such as 'truth, goodness, love, playfulness, beauty, unity, honesty, vitality and justice. Maslow called these the 'b-values' which represent the values of 'being' in a higher, transpersonal (beyond the self) way. Maslow lists quite a few more and as with all lists, there is personal feeling and meaning involved for each reader. What would you consider to be your b-values?

Transcendence

Self-actualisation:
acheiving one's personal potential and self-awareness...

Esteem:
social value, self-esteem, personal accomplishment...

Belonging/love:
intimate relationships, friends, family...

Safety:
security of self, resources and health...

Physiological:
air, food, water, warmth, homeostasis, sex, sleep...

As with all models and theories, there is room for interpretation, overlap and fluidity of needs at different stages in life and under changing circumstances however, this model has sustained as a very useful tool for self-reflection and personal development since it's conception in 1943.

Consider for yourself... are any of your needs not being met? If so, what are they? Can you identify what's missing and take action to remedy this? For example: do you feel alone in this world? Do you feel physically unsafe? Do you feel at risk from illness?

This is the perfect time to ask for support from others. In asking for help and assistance, you actually empower both yourself (your needs will be met allowing you movement upward) and, the other person is empowered in their need for self-esteem because you are giving the opportunity for significance and social value.

Beautiful.

Now, *what if...*

Where it seems obvious that Anxiety is a *response* to an unmet need (such as a lack of physical security), what if your Anxiety is also simultaneously *serving* or satiating *another* need? Sneaky, eh?!

Wouldn't this also become a strange and even addictive cycle?

Perhaps in response to feeling unsafe at the physiological level we orient around being 'responsible' - with safety controls, measures and checks - and in turn this satiates our need for personal significance and/or closeness with others as we become the 'safeguarder', protector or even rescuer.

What is your *Anxiety response to your needs* telling you? Are you perhaps, in a thoroughly ironic way, also trying to fulfil or satiate an unmet need with your anxious behaviours?

Could there be a better, growth-oriented way to meet these needs instead?

If you want stronger relationships or enhanced significance, perhaps it's time to take positive risks - open up to others and allow deeper bonds to form. In this example, where 'responsibility' is the suitable modus operandi, we could consider instead that allowing ourselves to feel vulnerable might actually be a strength. Now I know this sounds counter-intuitive: vulnerability as a strength!?

Whaaaaaat?!

For now, consider that it is simply the other side of the proverbial control coin, and we will come on to this in detail later.

Negative Automatic Thoughts

We often experience a fast-flowing stream of *racing thoughts*, belligerent repeating *intrusive thoughts*, or what therapists love to call 'your NATs' - *Negative Automatic Thoughts* - those dark, undermining thoughts that seem to just pop into your head to make you feel like crap.

Whichever way we experience them we assume they hold a value of 'truth', even if we 'know' that they do not. Ironic, right? Yes. Accept that it so and you can be released from their grip. Wrestle with them and you give them your attention, time, and energy.

NATs and intrusive thoughts are those unwanted thoughts that seem to self-start the Anxiety cycle. They suddenly and unexpectedly appear in your awareness - like a coughing fit does in your lungs - it catches you by surprise and dominates all other thoughts and bodily attention. That is, until you stop coughing. They are annoying 'brain coughs'.

Thoughts like: *"Have I left the iron on?"*

Now, having safety thoughts is normal, and even healthy, and if it was just this thought then our reasonable brain could just say 'no', and that would be the end of it. Unfortunately, Anxiety will not let the matter drop and must dominate the argument with all sorts of unhelpful, irrational thinking styles like *emotional reasoning* and *catastrophising*. For example, where Anxiety has set up camp, the above thought becomes less of a practical reasonable question and more like a series of increasingly elaborate horror scenarios delivered by a toddler in meltdown:

Scenario A: "Have I left the iron on?... No, it is off, I unplugged it like always. Besides if there was a problem its thermostat would kick in and shut it off - and failing that the fuse in the plug would blow."

But then Anxiety joins the conversation.

Anxiety - "Hmm, but of course IF it is still on then you are mistaken and so there is reason to doubt *all* your reasoning. In fact, if it is on, it might catch fire and cause everyone in the house to be killed and maybe even the next house too. Also have you even considered how bad you would feel? Let us imagine the suffering, the funerals, the tabloid headlines that would show you responsible saying 'all because she never checked the iron was off'."

Scenario B: "What if a spider peeps into my glass of water whilst I'm sleeping?" You might even have a rationalising conversation with yourself, as though your reasoning brain and Anxiety play out two aspects of your sitcom self:

Anxiety: "Psst, hey. It is me. I was just wondering... What if a spider peeps into our glass of water whilst we're sleeping?"

Brain: "What?"

Anxiety: "Yeh, *What if...?*"

Brain: "Go to sleep. You are being ridiculous."

Anxiety: You're not listening. I will create a series of implausible but highly detailed mental images to illustrate my concern..."

Ok, so there is no rational reason to now deprive yourself of sleep or useful function but what if...?

Here is a little anecdote that shows a good example of how to 'flip your negative' - and just how effective it can be.

It was a few years ago now and I will never forget it. I was sitting writing up notes in a wellbeing centre when the mother of a 7 year-old child I had only met for 5 minutes the previous day, called me for a 'frank talk'... (gulp!).

Mother: "I want to know what you said to my daughter."

Me: "Certainly, may I ask who your daughter is please?"

(necessary preamble...)

Mother: "Whatever it was, she is a different girl now. She slept all night in her own bed for the first time and today, she woke up sunny and smiling. She is a totally different child. Thank you."

Me: *(massive sigh of relief and the urge to pee, passing...)* "Oh, I see, she shared with me that she got very upset whenever she saw an emergency service vehicle - or heard a siren. That she imagined all sorts of terrible things."

I suggested that next time she saw or heard one, she could instead think this:

'Isn't that absolutely marvellous?! Oh my, what a wonderful thing! That all those people have trained their whole lives to care for others, just when we might need help. That some clever person has built those very special vehicles and that we have a whole system to deliver the best help to anyone who wants it - and all we have to do is dial three little numbers. How amazing is that?! How lucky are we to have this?!'

I asked her to imagine the people smiling and helping, being kind and grateful - even *enjoying* their roles. That it was ok to feel anxious, because it showed she cared and, that she could choose to experience it as excitement for the hope it brings - instead of sleepless worry.

I remember watching her little face as she shared the idea. She went from tense to relaxed and looked thoughtful.

I had no idea she had had her own epiphany.

Now the reason I was able to deliver this on the spot is very simple. Empathy. It was also my own epiphany one day not so long ago because I used to have the same Anxiety over the emergency service vehicles too. Now I don't.

Typical Behaviours

Anxious behaviours are things we do and, also the things we *do not* do, motivated by those thoughts, emotions, and physical sensations and, are generally all about perceived safety. For example:

Avoidance

Where you avoid going out so you can avoid seeing someone in particular or maybe people in general. Where you avoid opening your mail so you can avoid having to deal with bills. Where you avoid talking to anyone (except the cat as they are great listeners) because you want to avoid owning up to a problem and/or avoid crying and maybe also feeling embarrassed.

Compulsions/Rituals

These are things we do to 'neutralise' the intrusive thoughts and make up the 'C' in Obsessive Compulsive Disorder (OCD). We often ritualise our compulsive behaviour to give us the sense of control and predictability that we crave.

Typical compulsions include hand-washing, tapping or flicking with fingers in certain numbers and of course, safety checking and reassurance seeking. For example, where you check that doors are locked to avoid intrusion. Where you check in with others to check they are cool with you (and that you haven't unwittingly destroyed your relationship and not realised). Where you check appliances are off and not going to burn your house down. Where you check that said appliances are unplugged in case they turn rogue, turn themselves on, turn against you - and burn your house down.

This one is close to my heart (or should I say brain?) as I used to perform elaborate safety checks day and night. I even became fixated on hair straighteners that I rarely ever used and would go back to the bedroom many times to check they were off. It got worse and where I'd left for the day I would sometimes do a 180 degree turn after 5 minutes travel and go back to the house to check again.

During this time, I heard a man on television say that to help control his safety-based OCD he took his iron with him in the car to work every day. I remember thinking that this man was a GENIUS, I was all 'give that man the Nobel Prize for Anxiety!'.

Duly impressed I began taking electrical appliances with me too. However, on one occasion I *still* went back home to check the hair straighteners were off, only to panic when I couldn't find them. They were in the car of course, still a little warm, resting comfortably in the passenger seat like a harmless snoozing kitten. I felt erm, rather daft.

In reality, this kind of behaviour actually reinforces the Anxiety because it is participating in a cycle of ritualised behaviour to neutralise the intrusive thought. Also, the practical aspect of taking an appliance with you kind of goes out the window when you start worrying about your white goods. I don't imagine I could have managed the tumble dryer in my car every morning.

Aggression

Being irritable, snappy and even aggressive is common. Rising stress hormones leaves us full of undirected energy, ready to fight with a sense of urgency. Being a snappy turtle to those around us or even harbouring aggressive thoughts can also compound the negative cycle of feeling bad ourselves and on edge about out worrisome thoughts.

When we feel we have no control and that our sense of agency is stifled, it's perfectly understandable that we might be overwhelmed. Being anxious is exhausting work and sometimes if only others around us could know that and anticipate our needs we might feel supported. Of course, unless we ask for help this is all unfair wishful thinking that anyone can and ought to be helping.

Perfectionism

This is a sneaky one. We are in many ways fed the peculiar idea that perfectionism is a good thing - that somehow it means we have 'higher standards' than others but it just isn't true. It is not helpful nor healthy as perfection can never be achieved. Perfectionism is an expression of Anxiety where a person fears their performance will be 'substandard' and lead to shame, rejection, danger and so on. It leads to exhausting and destructive behaviour for example, spending hours checking and re-checking things like email content before sending, personal grooming and presentation, organising our homes and workspaces to an impossibly high and ultimately unattainable standard. It interferes with our relationships with others as we cannot let go of things we are responsible for - which has a knock on effect of efficiency of work flow, time management, social interaction and self-care.

Hoarding

No time like the present pandemic to become acutely aware of the connection between hoarding and Anxiety. When news broke of the virus, here in the UK people went crazy for buying up certain items. Some seemed to make a kind of sense such as paracetamol, hand-sanitiser and anti-bacterial house cleaner. However, the mentality spilled over in to catastrophising that food and general supplies would become a scarcity as though in some kind of apocalyptic movie, and the people of Britain went out and cleared the shelves of all the dried pasta - and loo roll! Pasta and loo roll have become interesting symbols of what we obviously value as a culture - Italian food and not being 'caught short' in the toilet.

Hoarding is often a difficulty in letting go of objects where the person emotionally attaches to the things. It can also be an expression of fear of being unprepared, that by discarding or recycling things, you might find yourself in a perilous deficit and need of those items in a future scenario. It doesn't matter that the objects being hoarded may be obscure, such as newspapers, wonky cutlery, empty jam jars, ancient copies of Horse & Hound magazine, coat hangers, empty crisp packets, that printer that never worked, expired spices, clothes that don't fit, empty cardboard boxes, broken appliances, broken watches and clocks, broken toys and in a more philosophical way, broken dreams and broken promises - we certainly struggle to let those go.

Of course, many of us are 'collectors' and there may well be a fine line between collecting and hoarding. Hoarding is a compulsion and the items are generally stored in a chaotic way. I'd argue that as long as we are mindfully curating our collections to 'give us joy' as Marie Kondo would say, and not to become an obsessive need that might leave us overwhelmed or in financial crisis, then we don't need to start worrying that we are in denial of hoarding.

Can you add to this list? I bet you 10p and a biscuit and a nice coconut thing *and* a bag of chips that you can.

How are you wired up?

As we repeat our thoughts and actions, over and over we increase the likelihood of them occurring. Just like treading a familiar pathway every day with our feet, we also create routes or neural pathways in our brains that lead to a kind of 'automated' reactive experience of the world. Through repetition, we manifest our expectations. This is the concept of 'neuroplasticity' - it literally means that we can shape and reshape our neurology. The biggest piece of news here is that we can *choose* what we want the outcomes to be. We can 'wire' ourselves for success, for health, for joy...

As Donald Hebb (a 20th century neuroscientist) famously

said, *"Neurons (cells) that fire together, wire together."* and many scientists, therapists and practitioners from a huge variety of specialisms today, also hold this to be true. This goes for an anxious person being 'wired' for the 'fight or flight' response just as much as a bold person being wired for success.

We can choose our interpretation of physical sensations, our thoughts and our behaviours.

We kind of 'strengthen' the reality of our experiences at the cellular level where cells and neurons influence one another in a series of activation and excitement - like an electrical circuit passing energy around. Where repeated, a kind of fusion takes place and our brains and bodies are 'rewired' to the purpose we intend.

> *"Progress is the victory of a new thought over old superstitions."*
> **Elizabeth Cady Stanton**

We could choose the happiness, wellness and self-esteem we want - in place of the previous NATs that we assumed we were lumped with. In fact, the negative wiring we don't want can be left inactivated to simply atrophy. Reinforcing what we want by repetition (e.g. with mantras, positive affirmations, self-care, positive actions) whilst we abandon what we don't want, is as simple as 'use it or lose it'. Now there's a mantra in itself.

In consideration of neuroplasticity *as a practice*, I asked the very lovely Diane Webb, (psychotherapist, Licensed Mental Health Counsellor) to share her experience of working with it. She says: *"When you are intentionally creating a new neural connection AWAY from an old, unhealthy one, it is very challenging and requires focused effort. Imagine driving down a highway and exiting off and onto a dirt road. That is the intentional effort and focus that is required to change this anxious neural network. The key is to focus your attention and continue to exit again and again until the dirt road is so well-travelled that it becomes a part of the paved, smooth highway as well."*

So, wiring is a choice. Think about what gets you *fired up* in life - and (re)wire for that.

What wiring do you choose (and choose to lose)?

A few notes on disorders

Disordered Anxiety of course can take many forms and in the notes here I am giving a brief erm 'brief' for the sake of brevity - so that we can move on to working on and transcending through our personal experiences.

It is important to note that Anxiety as a general experience is totally normal, in fact a very important part of the overall *human experience*, however, it is considered a *'disorder'* when it interferes significantly with daily life and happiness. If you feel that this is you (or someone close to you) then perhaps clinical treatment can help. I urge you to consult your doctor or mental health professional - and *please* speak candidly about what you are experiencing.

I've been there too and I can tell you this: it's absolutely ok to feel awkward or shy or even adverse to seeking help - this is ironically part of the anxious experience where we want to 'control' it ourselves, and the very idea of admitting we might benefit from support makes us feel... anxious. I've been down this route of avoidance myself. I eventually asked for support from my GP after many stubborn years of refusing to do so despite 'knowing' I needed to address an escalating problem. The upshot was that a combination of low intensity therapy and some pharmacology gave me the 'breathing space' to address my experience of worry and accompanying low mood. In fact, worry and low mood often go together - like a pair of really crappy shoes that won't let you walk forward.

Here is a very brief outline of some common Anxiety disorders. They can take many forms, are experienced differently by different people and are diagnosed by a mental health professional or family doctors. Here are some of the more common forms:

Generalised Anxiety

Generalised Anxiety Disorder (GAD) is a general prevailing state of tension and excessive worry that interferes with a person's day to day life through being unable to focus on tasks. GAD experiencers tend to be worrying every day, all day and often all night too leading to additional sleep disorders.

It is a long-term condition that does not apply specifically to any one worry and so is hard to pinpoint and understand. It's also considered to be quite a common disorder affecting approximately 5% of the UK public, affecting middle-aged women as the main demographic.

Panic Attacks

Panic attacks are an intensified concentrated experience of Anxiety triggered by fear and the switch-on of the 'fight or flight response' releasing adrenaline often with a horrifying 'sense of impending doom'. They can come on suddenly and are utterly

overwhelming. We all experience Anxiety as a normal part of the human condition. It is an unconscious defence mechanism preparing us for potential threat - when relevant. However, when Anxiety is misfiring like a machine gun having a seizure, it can lead to panic attacks and here, it has earned itself a special place as the world's worst superhero (or perhaps antihero is more apt) with the unique superpowers of hysterical problematic invention that only you can see.

Panic Attacks can feel like a person is having a heart attack and the fear of that compounds the situation further. Identifying that it is a panic attack and that it will be short-lived is helpful in enduring this state. The adrenal system pumps for about 20 minutes and then exhausts itself so, knowing that this will be temporary allows the experiencer to manage better in the moment.

Of course, the sensations as described in before (shaky legs, pounding heart, tight chest, sweating, dizziness, etc.) take longer to dissipate and the experience leaves a person totally energetically wiped out.

Health Anxiety

Health Anxiety takes the form of persistent worries about health and illness. Experiencers tend to be caught up in excessive self-examination looking for changes in skins tone, lumps and bumps, they may count their pulse and keep track of it. They may be noticing different sensations such as itches, heat or tingling within the body - and interpreting them as 'symptoms of illness'.

They obsessively looking up 'symptoms' in books and online, seeking reassurance from others and frequent trips to see their doctors. They may also behave as though they are ill with particular illnesses and, experience genuine pain or discomfort despite there being no physical cause detected.

Interestingly, as we will see later in the book, our beliefs and our bodies work together to manifest very real cures and curses - and we can take control of this for our benefit.

Social Anxiety

Social Anxiety is a long-term problem for experiencers who are deeply anxious about social situations. Social situations take many forms including everyday activities like talking on the phone, shopping or standing at a bus stop with strangers.

It interferes in the social life and development of the individual as they avoid parties, eating with others and family gatherings - opportunities that would usually nourish their sense of belonging.

People with Social Anxiety tend to fear that they will embarrass themselves or others and worry that they are being observed and judged all the time. Panic Attacks are common for people to experience when in these situations which of course, reinforces the desire to avoid social situations.

Specific Phobias

Phobias are irrational fears that can prevent people doing certain tasks as they avoid contact with the object of their fear. Common phobias often focus on safety.

Interestingly, some phobias can arise off the back of other Anxiety problems including agoraphobia (fear of the 'marketplace', typically meaning public spaces) which can manifest the more a person avoids going out for other reasons.

Whether that's spiders, crowds, aeroplanes, buttons or clowns, phobias are often obscure or peculiar and unlikely to cause daily problems, but others are completely disabling because the object is commonplace or necessary in day to day life, e.g. being afraid of people with beards (pogonophobia). I once knew a children's entertainer who was frantically afraid of balloons (globophobia), she became a dog groomer instead.

Obsessive Compulsive Disorder (OCD)

Obsessive thoughts and compulsive behaviour that includes having intrusive upsetting thoughts (e.g. contamination or harmful accidents) and the resulting compulsion to perform a ritualised action (e.g. excessive hand washing and safety checks) that 'neutralises' the thought. OCD can show up in many ways such as hoarding, checking (you can review my own experience of this in the previous section on typical behaviours) and can be spotted easily when ritualised behaviour can be observed.

A Quick look at CBT

When I was at university studying for my Psychology degree nearly 20 years ago, I was stunned by the elegance and efficacy of the CBT approach we learned about. Unbeknown to me then, I would go on to personally benefit from it ten years later and so I feel it's important to touch on it here.

The Cognitive Behavioural Therapy (CBT) approach, pioneered by that same Aaron Beck of distortion fame, looks mainly at our *thoughts, behaviours,* and *physical 'symptoms'* (but we will call them 'sensations').

It looks at the relationship between our cognitions (worried thoughts), behaviours (things we do or avoid) and physical sensations (e.g. heart racing, sweating, nausea and so on) and looks for vicious cycles to break typically in the behavioural zone. For example, perhaps yours might look like this:

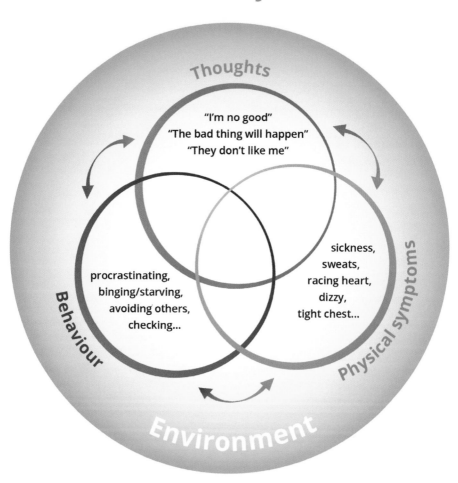

Try mapping it for yourself on this blank one

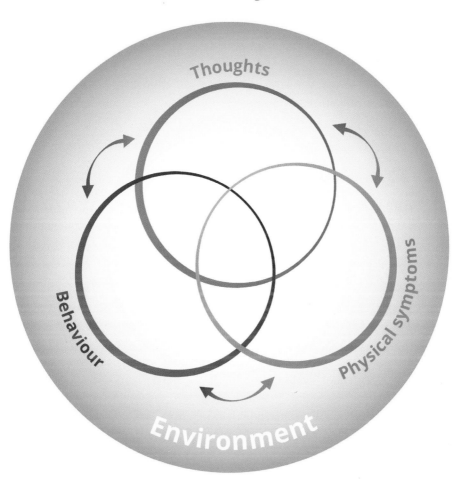

Notice too that there is another element to consider on these diagrams - the 'environment'.

Our environments are in themselves often triggers. For example, perhaps your Anxiety appears when you are at work or more specifically, when in meetings. Perhaps it's by the side of the stage before a performance. Perhaps it occurs in social situations or when travelling. Maybe it's at home, in a specific place or in the company of certain others.

Consider the following:

- When does it most often arise?
- Where are you?
- Who is there?
- What is the situation?

Furthermore, think about how objects and things in your environment reflect your worries and negative messages back to you. For example, an abandoned gym bag or dusty musical instrument might be saying 'hey, you failed at me...'. Or, your clothes might be commenting on your weight. Perhaps your unwashed dishes are criticising your domestic management skills or your cluttered desk at work is yelling at you with an impossible 'to-do' list.

Notice not only the thoughts about what messages they convey but also how you feel when you look at things in your environment. Are any physical sensations coming up? If so, where in the body? What emotions are rising? Are you feeling compelled to act in a certain way (e.g. hide the thing, hide all the things, hide yourself?)?

Morgana McCabe Allan, Ph.D, interdisciplinary expert in how

our reality emerges from our interactions with the world around us, says...

"Our reality and identity emerge through a co-creative process with the material world. We don't only create things to do what we want, that support our beliefs - we believe what our things feed back to us, do what they demand us to do (how often have you picked up your phone today?) We buy into the reality they promote - the entire global economy depends on it. What does that mean? Every single thing we interact with - whether we know it or not - elicits an embodied response. From an improvement in wellbeing associated with passing by brightly coloured masonry to the frustration of computers loading at slow speeds, objects are acting back upon us. Every energy has agency. If we want to create new realities, we have to be very intentional in exactly which places, people, things and ideas we co-create with. Wherever we put attention - even if it is to dispute merit - we are giving power. Attention does mean, after all, to extend towards."

Core **Blimey! We are of more value than the sum of our parts!**

So, what does this all mean? How do we go beyond the C, the B, and the T? How do we stop being a bunch of parts in conflict, and learn to be one united being?

Firstly, you must recognise that none of your sensations are bigger than You. The whole experience is not 'in charge'. You are the one *having* the multifaceted experience, which will pass. The experience is happening *within* you, not *to* you by some external force, nor can it take over you - because you are creating it.

So... in taking Anxiety as a positive 'whole' and not fixating on the negative parts, how do I find this inner guru? To do this you firstly need to accept that Anxiety is an individual experience, and that each different person will experience different symptoms. Anxiety is the manifestation of some hidden 'doubt' - and your mind and body are telling you about the problem. It is just hard to listen clearly sometimes, especially when your brain is trying to hog all the action and take charge of it all as a solely mental experience, to be analysed and shelved like an old textbook. It is crucial to consider that the other organs have a 'felt' wisdom to impart to you too.

We think of Anxiety as being 'made up of' our unhelpful thoughts, things we do or don't do, our physical sensations and how we feel emotionally, yet we tend to take each 'part' as though it stands alone. With all this in mind (yet it is also in our bodies), it is time to look more closely at our experience of Anxiety.

Our emotions are reactions to what's going on - in the world around us and also our inner world of thoughts, behaviour and sensations. Emotions inform us of our deep and often unconscious *core values*. Core values are those personal values that drive us (e.g. open-mindedness, family connections, vitality, kindness, creativity, justice, musicality, learning...). They are in our blueprint for being and doing.

Our individual core values are the things we want to honour with our lives and also at the same time, they are the values that challenge us the most. When we are angry, afraid or upset it is often because our core values are being challenged. In Anxiety, our emotional reactions are telling us an enormous amount about who we really are, at our core.

There are hundreds of words to describe core values and an easy way to work out what they are for us individually is to reflect on highs and lows in life - times when we have been ecstatic, utterly joyful or by contrast, enraged or devastated. Here we can begin to tease out the what, where, when, with whom... and ask ourselves *why* we felt how we did.

The '5 Whys' technique (established by car manufacturer Toyota in the 1930s for problem solving) is really useful in refining our understanding. In the case here of mining our values, we are basically thinking of an emotional high or low and asking 'why' it was the case. For example;

Situation: The time I was rejected from formal ballet school on medical grounds.

Emotion: Sadness, loneliness, self-loathing.

1. *Why was this rejection from a specific ballet school a problem?*
   It meant my body was 'wrong' for a life in ballet.

2. *Why was being 'wrong' for a life in ballet a problem?*
   It meant that what I wanted wasn't accessible to me.

3. *Why was this inaccessibility to a life in ballet a problem?*
   Because I was defining my worth according to acceptance in ballet.

4. *Why was defining my worth according to acceptance in ballet a problem?*
   Because it limited me.

5. *Why was being limited a problem?*
   Because I want to GROW.

There are many ways to grow

Such limitations are self-imposed. They are beliefs. They manifest through the obscuring lenses of what we 'think' makes us acceptable and lovable by others, in any given moment. One of my core values is social *inclusion* and another is *growth*. Coincidence? I would come to repeat this cycle many times in my life and yet, each time I am motivated to challenge the status quo for the benefit of myself and, I'm pleased to say others too.

Similarly, consider asking yourself 'What if...' 5 times to get to see the many amazing other potential realities you could be inhabiting. What if... a life changing event you fear actually holds the motivation you seek?

For example:

What if... *not getting ahead in your job is an opportunity for new adventure?*

- What if this means you are actually free to choose your direction?
- What if you go somewhere totally new and exciting?
- What if this brings new people into your life?
- What if one of those people offers you the chance of a lifetime?
- ...?

What if... *having an illness could bring a benefit for you? What would that look like?*

- What if the change in lifestyle creates room for a new healing passion?
- What if that passion leads you to heal?
- What if your healing journey inspires others?
- What if you become a healer?
- ...?

What if... not having a degree in fine art makes you a more interesting artist?

- What if by breaking the established pro-forma you stand out?
- What if by standing out you become very successful?
- What if in becoming successful as an 'outsider' you become a teacher?
- What if in becoming this teacher you define a whole new movement?
- ...?

It's all about choosing how you perceive life changes and transitions.

Emotion - the guiding light within

Do you get annoyed when others say, "you are too sensitive" or "overly emotional"? Well, have you ever heard a research scientist complain about having too much information? The problem is not in an instrument's sensitivity, it is in the user's skill of filtering useful information.

Philosophers and psychologists have debated and discussed the nature of emotions for eons. Some say they are caused by the body, others that they exist independently of physicality, some regard them as the building blocks of our experience, others as accidental phenomenon. Jean-Paul Sartre argued that in a way, our emotions are strategies that we do - ways we interact with the world. in negative emotions, where we feel we do not have control, they are acts in which we try to escape from difficult situations. E.g. Resentment is an act that allows us to escape responsibility such as when we fail to pass a test we think "oh well that test is only for XY or Z types anyway" ... I think that so too is Anxiety. It allows us to escape that feeling we cannot tolerate - that feeling of not being in control. Acting in Anxiety, we start to mentally take control by 'preparing' for all eventualities. We think we are being pro*active* - rather than becoming exhausted with unnecessary mental action.

Freud elaborated that we enjoy or are attracted to horror as a kind of catharsis of hidden fear. Of course, fear is paradoxical. Fear is automatic and useful when there is a threat, but Anxiety is almost like a kind of fear that self generates where we are disengaged from information and instead rely on anticipated, hypothetical threat. I would argue that Anxiety is fear that is manifested by a combination of information and misinformation that are difficult to distinguish between.

To me, emotions are exquisite data about who we truly are. I can't say 'how' they come about in the same way that I can't answer how we came into being at all, but the 'how' isn't too important. Instead, I focus on emotions as the reactions we have at our core; reactions to what is going on in the world around us and also, in our inner worlds of thoughts and sensations too. They are meaningful information as well as being experiences in themselves. They are fluid, changing and transformational reflections of our soul.

Emotions are the Inner Compass

I think that the late Robert Solomon (luminary professor of philosophy and author) put it beautifully when he said *"Emotions are the key to the meaning of life"*.

As well as being a guiding light like a torch we carry that illuminates us, emotions are also giving us direction. They are highly nuanced acts of consciousness that show us how we interact with the world; influenced by our moods, conceptual awareness, and core values.

Emotions are dynamic - both acting on and responding to our life experiences. So, for each of us, emotions are individually cultivated making them so very personal - and often tricky to accurately discuss.

Thinking a little more on the nature of emotions we can consider them to be different from feelings although they contain feelings - often a myriad or blend of feelings (e.g. butterflies in the tummy can be found in both joy and fear). Feelings can be physical responses - we feel heartache and churning tummies, but these are sensations associated with or perhaps resulting from our emotions. It can be easy to confuse or misinterpret feelings, e.g. excitement can be good or bad. It is all 'arousal'. By contrast, emotions tend to have an intelligence and involve concepts that allows us to evaluate things - e.g. 'I am angry because I was lied to' or 'I am proud because I tried something new today'. We can determine certain truths or falsehoods about lies and achievements. Emotions have a moral compass.

Moods too, are different. Moods can last from mere moments to lifetimes. Like weather in our external environment, moods are our overall internal environment - which colour and influences our perspective and subjective experience of the world. Come rain, shine, stormy times, and dark clouds, we all appreciate a rainbow - that phenomena that represents hope, reminding us to perceive the light.

What makes emotions special is that they also give us insight on how to act. They represent our desires and are active experiences - things that we 'do' so that we may respond to, process, and use our life experiences. It is through the guidance of our emotions that we can come to 'know thyself' and work on self-improvement.

Feelings, emotions, and moods are responses to the world, but emotions are also active roles that we consciously *do*.

Thoughts, behaviours and physical sensations tend to lead to these experiences called 'emotions' and we perceive them as energy - they are vibrations felt within the body. Emotions are impermanent and change from one to another - they transform and transmute, changing their guidance according to changes around us, like an excellent GPS system. The trick is to notice, appreciate and value what they tell you when you feel them. Also, notice when they are absent, when they emerge and also when they change from one to another in often a very contrasting way.

Let's think again on where emotions are 'felt' or experienced. They can be elusive but are very enlightening markers on our maps to self-discovery. We often talk about them as being physical, and they can be experienced as located in the body - e.g. in the heart we feel heartache, heavy heart, hearty laughter and so on. In our bones we can feel 'chilled' by some sinister force or we can 'feel' or 'know' something in our bones. Our skin can crawl in revulsion. We can have a sinking stomach and feel light-headed yet heavy footed. Our heads can also ache, and our brains can fog over when under stress. We feel emotions in our bodies, but we often default to trying to process them as either physical sensations of illness or as mental experiences to be analysed, and we override or even ignore the 'sensation' of them as they occur in the present moment.

The fundamental irony is that we 'think we know what we feel' and we 'feel we ought to know what we think' but we never just acknowledge the feelings as having any wisdom of their own. They are almost entirely validated by thoughts *about* them.

When we notice the emotional reaction to our thoughts, behaviours, or physical sensations we are being shown a clue as to what is really going on, where our values lie and what our 'truths' are. But this amazing inner wisdom is largely ignored or overruled.

Emotions are also like creative directors. They all have a vision and impact on our perception of reality. Joy, sadness, humour, fear... they all play specific instruments or roles in the big production that is You. They often fight for the limelight. But there is a quiet genius operating there too - *Intuition*.

That uncanny feeling that we are angling around some truth, epiphany, or revelation. It is the most subtle yet the most accurate of directors. Intuition can be felt in the gaps between other emotions and thoughts, suspended in the quiet.

Now here is another thoroughly 'iffy' point...

Intuition is (counter)intuitive

If something is counterintuitive, it is contrary to 'common sense' (or intuition). Ironically, when anxious it feels *counter*intuitive to trust our intuition.

This is because when we are anxious, we feel so much that we become overwhelmed. The voice of intuition is muffled by the voice of alarm. How often have you said or heard another say

"I KNEW something was up with that!" or "I had a funny feeling about her..." or "Argh, I totally knew that was going to happen".

Notice the past tense here. You see, all too often we only recognise intuition in hindsight. We ignore it at the time it would be useful because it feels *risky* to trust it. When we are anxious we are highly risk averse. We often ignore intuition, reasoning that we are 'being silly', unfair or that we do not have any evidence to back it up, that it is simply not 'rational', and we will regret listening to it.

The sense of irony is magnified again when we realise that by not trusting our intuition in favour of being risk averse, we are actually acting in a risky way! For example, a conversation between Anxiety and intuition might go like this:

Intuition: *"Hey, I have a funny feeling about Bob. Don't trust what he says about that car. It's a lemon."*

Anxiety: *"Hmm but what if you are wrong? What if you are being unfair to Bob?"*

Here, you feel bad for judging Bob and you worry you are a mean person *and* that you might miss an opportunity, so you allow yourself to be persuaded to buy a car you don't really want. To compound the problem further, each time you look at the car, your Anxiety is heightened as you know you really don't trust it to run well and begin to imagine it falling apart on the motorway.

So, if we are habitually ignoring our intuition, we need to act counterintuitively - to take the risk on ourselves, and learn to trust our intuition.

If this is tricky, remember that it's ok to notice if trusting your intuition feels risky. But it's a risk you are taking on *yourself.* You are in control because you are making a choice. Additionally, in doing this we glean a much bigger truth - that reality itself IS counterintuitive. Life, the universe, and everything is paradoxical.

Like any muscle, like any neuron, intuition is a 'use it or lose it' situation. We grow and strengthen our intuition by placing faith in it, by using it. This means taking risks on it. So, next time you notice that 'funny feeling' where you 'just know' something - and you also feel it's risky - take a punt and trust that counterintuition is simply flagging up the presence of intuition. Go against your feeling of avoidance, not against your intuition.

Emotional Intelligence

Emotional intelligence is generally considered to be about how well we recognise our own (and those of others) emotions and, how well we understand, manage, and use them to make decisions - in a useful way. Emotional intelligence has been found in many studies to be a significant predictor of health and happiness and, a far greater predictor of financial success than traditional 'IQ'. Considering that if emotions are a guiding light for personal truth, this makes complete sense because those emotions are helping you to make decisions which lead to action.

Our individual engagement with our world (our environment, other people, things we do) and also our internal world is made up of 'schemas', narratives or stories that we build. Now these stories we build - we live in - and as such are created in our own internal language, including the way we talk about our emotions. There is an important clue here for self-improvement and happiness, in that if we improve the quality of our emotional language, we improve our stories and we improve our wellbeing.

Those in love, see virtue and hope. Those in fear see threat. Those who are unhappy see futility and cruelty in the world. Just as we choose spectacles by the look and fit of the frame, and how the lens adjusts our reality we too can choose what emotional frame and lens we will look through and whether or not we will grow.

"Anxiety is there. It is only sleeping. Its breath quivers perpetually through Dasein, only slightly in those who are jittery, imperceptibly in the 'Oh, yes' and the 'Oh, no' of men of affairs; but most readily in the reserved, and most assuredly in those who are basically daring. But those daring ones sustained by that on which they expend themselves - in order thus to preserve the ultimate grandeur of existence."
Martin Heidegger

A little hack for indecision:

"What if I make the wrong decision?!"

How many of us are held back by this immobilising dark cloud?

There are no "wrong" nor "right" decisions - just decisions. Just action. Just you are doing, moving on in life's narrative. To live is to actively live through life, not sit immobile waiting for it to happen.

Since we cannot predict all the nuanced outcomes of any decision, we are deluded when we fear mistakes. There is only the now and how we handle it as it unfolds.

The truth is that you can handle whatever happens. In fact, unexpected situations are unexpected bonus opportunities to grow and learn and maybe even win the odds.

"What if...?"

"So what?"

Exercise - notice negative and destructive talk and consider flipping the language and perspective. Notice if you are taking anything "personally" or not as this leads to sophisticated differences e.g. between being apprehensive, full of trepidation, feeling nervous or feeling under threat. Or, feeling ashamed, guilty, or having regret. Or, like how we can laugh at both joyful or ironically, sad news - because when we receive a shock we often laugh as a kneejerk reaction (laughter isn't an emotion it's a reaction to something unexpected).

Notice - what am I experiencing? Name it!

Understand - where has it come from? Other modifying factors?

Manage - what do I want more/less of? What triggers and circumstances are there?

Use - what judgements have I been making? what am I learning about me? The world? Any changes? Am I saying it is one thing when it is actually another? Am I trying to hide something? (We often avoid recognising our own conceited attitudes and we also avoid letting others know we really feel resentment or fear).

"A depressed man lives in a depressed world."
Ludwig Wittgenstein

This taps into the concept that we 'create our realities'. We project our internal schemas and expectations on to the external world. Through our moods and attitudes, we manifest our experience. The lesson here is that we can CHOOSE whether we love or hate our experience of life.

Fear may be a 'basic emotion' - a universally found state of being that involves automatic neurological reactions. In terms of evolution it has served to motivate self-preservation. It is not the same as Anxiety. Anxiety tends to be 'about something' - it is nuanced and involves a lot of information (or misinformation) as a prerequisite, e.g. fearing a secret being disclosed, or the results of a medical test, or exam result...

Here, the 'whole' experience becomes 'holistic' and good, even spiritual, because our emotions are our reactions to things, including our own thoughts. Therefore, they tell us a huge amount about our values, needs, desires and our fears. Not as abstract as they might first seem, you physically feel emotions in your body - try to locate them physically when you bring up a certain emotion like love or fear or envy. Where do you feel them? What about intuition? It's a gut-feeling, right?

I feel (and think!) that with this extra dimension added in, the whole experience is greater than the sum of its unpleasant CB or T parts; and that working with our emotions is key to seeing this bigger picture. Our physical sensations are often our embodied emotions. If we draw upon the ancient Indian 'chakra system' of energy, we can better understand our needs - and direct our attention and energy to where it is needed. With this in our toolkit we can really envision the what, why and where we are experiencing emotions.

These centres or 'wheels' of energy (known as 'chakras') represent our state of being as embodied in 7 chakras represented in the light spectrum of colour going from the base of the spine (red) to the tops of our heads (violet). There are more chakras, but for our purposes in our IF journey, 7 is perfect.

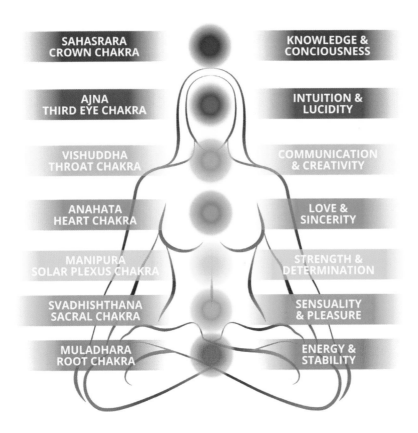

SAHASRARA
CROWN CHAKRA

KNOWLEDGE &
CONCIOUSNESS

AJNA
THIRD EYE CHAKRA

INTUITION &
LUCIDITY

VISHUDDHA
THROAT CHAKRA

COMMUNICATION
& CREATIVITY

ANAHATA
HEART CHAKRA

LOVE &
SINCERITY

MANIPURA
SOLAR PLEXUS CHAKRA

STRENGTH &
DETERMINATION

SVADHISHTHANA
SACRAL CHAKRA

SENSUALITY
& PLEASURE

MULADHARA
ROOT CHAKRA

ENERGY &
STABILITY

The chakras represent stages of human development - and therefore also our needs. When we feel something that aligns with a chakra position, it helps inform us of our lack or abundance in that area - i.e. what we need, and what is driving us.

Just like Maslow's hierarchy of needs, the chakra system shows a flow that ideally requires each chakra point to be fulfilled at each stage before real progress can be made 'up' the spine and beyond.

Here is a very brief look at the Chakras and how they might inform us of where our attention needs to go:

Red: *Base (or Root) Chakra*
Located right at the base of the spine and genital area.
Relates to our feelings of basic survival, energy and safety.

Orange: *Sacral Chakra*
Located at our abdomen area.
Relates to sexuality, social being, pleasure.

Yellow: *Solar Plexus Chakra*
Located at the solar plexus area.
Relates to personal power, agency, personality.

Green: *Heart Chakra*
Located at the heart area.
Relates to love, sincerity, compassion.

Blue: *Throat Chakra*
Located at the throat area.
Relates to communication, creativity, self-expression.

Indigo: *Third Eye Chakra*
Located in the head between the eyebrows.
Relates to intuition, clarity, self-trust.

Violet: *Crown Chakra*
Located on top/just above of the head.
Relates to expanded consciousness, spirituality, transcendence.

Relating to the Chakras is a personal practice. They are your Chakras and they are part of the overall symbiotic system that is you. Often in Anxiety, the Root Chakra is key, where a person does not feel safe or secure. Working on this area (visualising the colour red filling and nourishing this area of your body and whole body in turn) will bring about feelings of enhanced security. Not only will this help relieve the unpleasant feelings but as you visualise improving you will prompt yourself to take aligned *action*. Upon identifying a need that requires satisfying you will begin to seek out the support and changes you require.

Other examples include where tight sensations in your throat might indicate that your needs for being heard and understood are not being met. A pain in your solar plexus might suggest that you are feeling disempowered.

Headaches could be telling you that there is a lack of trust in your life. I highly recommend getting better acquainted with this and in practising awareness of the Chakras as you ideally meditate or rest.

Our emotions are also not subject to linear time as they manifest in response to real or imagined events inside your mind now or in the past or imagined future. They could be memories, present tense or future imaginings.

But here is the really useful thing... They are your personal internal moral compass - they tell you how you are responding to events in both the external world and our internal thoughts and sensations.

Why is this important? **They tell you about your core values.**

For example:

- When you hear that a child is been bullied, do you feel angry? Hurt? Where do you feel it in your body? What does this tell you about your values? Why are you feeling this there?

- When you imagine your future-self looking at your lovely published book or artwork hanging in the gallery of your dreams, what do you feel? Pride? Excitement? Joy? Where do you feel it in your body? Why there? What does this suggest to you?

Similarly, intrusive thoughts (persistent upsetting thoughts) can make us feel awful as though we are terrible people. E.g. thoughts of harm, death, suffering, inappropriate sexual or social thoughts about gender roles, race or class.

However, these are just thoughts - they are mental events happening within you, they are not YOU.

I once heard of a man who marched every campaign he could for equal rights and yet he was plagued with intrusive thoughts of a racist nature. He felt awful, as though these thoughts meant he was a secret racist and a fraud.

Of course, the irony was that in being so utterly devastated by these thoughts he failed to see that his emotional reaction was proof of his being quite the opposite! The thoughts were not any kind of truths, instead the emotional reaction *to* the thoughts was enlightening.

If you have persistent upsetting thoughts, what are they? What emotion occurs in response? Where in the body is it located? What is this telling you about your needs?

Here, we can start to consider the 'Big Questions', those enormous concepts that underpin our mindset, attitudes, expectations and overall experience of life.

By identifying where and when those 'big questions' are prompting the experience of Anxiety, and in noticing our emotional responses as we go (that 'inner compass'), then we can uncover our truths and nourish our personal growth. After all,

Anxiety is physically the same as excitement - but the experience we have is decided by the mental interpretation.

The BIG Questions

Listening to our emotions, especially intuition, helps us to uncover answers to these with a sense of interconnectedness. Essentially, how we respond unconsciously (as also demonstrated in our behaviours) is based on how we perceive and interpret the world around us and we can take the self-discoveries in hand for closer examination.

Consider - what can we learn from our thoughts, behaviours, and physical sensations about what we *really* think, feel, and believe about the big questions underneath?

The Little Worries are the BIG Questions

We all have underlying Anxiety about the BIG existential questions: who am I? What is the point of living? What happens when we die? Where did we come from? Is there a God? These questions begin in childhood and never win satisfaction and so anxious children and anxious adults are very similar at heart. We never grow up in this respect - at best, we just learn to 'manage' these fears and doubts with an accumulation of stories. Many of these stories are unconvincing at best and the resulting mistrust or doubt adds to our feelings of uncertainty.

As the stories build so do our core beliefs (those beliefs that lie deep within, unconsciously sleeping under the weight of everything else we think and feel). We also begin to build barriers and defences against them stirring and waking up and so we never learn to inspect, challenge or augment them. We don't grow.

Ironically, they still pop up as 'the little things' that keep us awake at night: Have I left the iron on? Was that hairy looking sausage safe to eat? Should I ask for a pay rise like Lorna? Am I too fat for those purple yoga pants? Are my kids 'normal'? How many cats make a crazy cat lady? and so on...

Self-Experiment:

Have you ever noticed that when you ask questions in your own head, that there is an immediate 'other voice' that answers back, but, for some reason, you totally ignore it? It is as though you dismiss the answers in favour of the questions. Try it now... ask yourself a question and then pause as you notice the answer and linger on it.

What did you ask?

What was the response?

You don't have to agree to the response - it's not necessarily 'correct' but what it is, is a starting point for answering the very question you asked but more importantly, the BIG ones that lie beneath.

Your Comfort Zones are making you Uncomfortable

Comfort zones are more like *discomfort* zones. What if your perceived comfort is the very thing that creates your discomfort with your lot in life?

There is an uncomfortable truth lurking in the shadows of our comfort zones: they are more self-made prisons than the personal playgrounds or protective bubbles we like to think. Despite its name, your comfort zone isn't necessarily a comfortable or happy place. Some people are comfortable residing in a space of intolerance, anger or self-pity; others even seem to thrive in an environment of high stress. Many people refuse to leave such spaces - despite being miserable.

So, why does recognising the boundaries of our comfort zones matter? Self-esteem.

We are not born with self-esteem; we grow it through positive risk-taking adventures. Through babyhood, childhood, teenage years and for the rest of our lives. As babies, children and young adults we need to be nurtured - *encouraged to grow.* We need to be encouraged to take those risks to reap the rewards of discovering our own abilities and to do so knowing that we have support - going to nursery for the first time, making a new friend, holding a scary snake or petting a big dog for the first time, auditioning for a play, trying a contact sport, riding a bike and so on.

> *"We make ourselves in the things we do."*
> **Morgana McCabe Allan, Ph.D**

So, the same for adults - we need peer and familial support and new positive risk-taking adventures. When we are not nurtured (or simply refuse to be nurtured as many do), and put up barriers or defences, we end up walled into a comfort zone of fear. We think the walls protect us but they simply keep us captive to our own imagined demons.

We cling to our comfort zones typically because therein we have familiarity and predictability. Even if what is familiar and predictable is uncomfortable - anyone who has been stuck in an abusive marriage for years will tell you exactly that - they were stuck.

Force is needed to overcome the stuck-ness. This is why the decision to take a risk is crucial. The risk is the force that is needed.

Think about all the times you have said to yourself "here I go again", or you've felt that your career, relationships, decisions and life in general is going around in circles? That life is on a loop? Often one that feels exhausting and frustrating? Well, maybe it is. Maybe it's a feedback loop of what you are thinking and doing resulting in the same things over and over and over... leading to the same experiences, over and over.

But what *IF...*? That loop is not what it seems and that by perceiving it differently, you can immediately and massively upscale your career, relationships, decisions and life in general?

It's just a matter of choice.

Loop v Spiral

What if...
it's not a loop...

...it's a spiral!

From a different angle

Each time we come around in the loop, we actually do so at a different point in time, as different people (we are older and have different experiences since the last time). What if we could super-charge that route so that the height and breadth of the spiral was expanding and growing us with each cycle round?

We can. We choose to do so by embracing the perspective and asking ourselves what do we learn each time and, what will we do more of and less of next? We can leave the old pattern behind - and not return to the same piss-poor frustrations because instead of looping around, we are going up, up, up and expanding out, out, out.

What do you need to make this simple yet fundamental change?

Answer: **Insight and action.**

What insight does Anxiety tell you about your values, your beliefs, your behaviour? What needs to change?

Let that change be *action*. Positive risk-taking.

Now of course, with risk comes well... risk. We often fear change and loss. Everything and everyone we love changes or leaves at some point or at many points, and so do we from the lives of others. Loss is difficult, but also a necessary part of growth beyond those comfort zones. We are all travelling intertwined spirals that see each of us arriving at or leaving a job, town or relationship to changes of career, lifestyle or mindset.

So, think of your loop as your restricting limiting comfort zone - and your spiral as your way up and out.

Oh, and that hole on the middle of the spiral, that 'gap' that also expands and grows up and out? Well, the gap is not empty. The gap is the expansive potential you are creating and drawing on simultaneously. You see? The 'stuff' in the middle of the spiral that looks like empty space is actually all the learning, all the choices, all the energy, all the connections - it is the ALL, the EVERYTHING you have created and will create.

As you expand and grow, so does it. Awesome, right? So, as long as you have momentum to keep moving *in alignment with your chosen positive direction,* your potential also grows with you, fuelling your growth. Forever.

Why stay 'stuck' expecting things to remain comfortably familiar? Surely this can only lead to Anxiety and resentment? Even the littlest positive change will result in change for the better.

With this in mind... What's it going to be? Loop or Spiral?

There is a difference between being uncomfortable and being in discomfort. Being uncomfortable suggests there is something with agency poking at or harming us in some causal way and to be in discomfort suggests a lack of that which comforts us. Ironically, they both hold space for the illusion of a comfort zone.

Until we move, take a risk and see what's beyond our boundaries we won't recognise either the agency responsible or what we lack, and we will continue to be our own captors. It's always time to push the boundaries, to step out and take positive risks.

Taking responsibility (too far) can be irresponsible

Keeping ourselves and each other in a bubble that doesn't actively explore contrasting ideas, address taboo or try to understand differing values is *avoidance* behaviour. It may feel counterintuitive to expose ourselves and others to risk but if we don't, we do them - and their futures - a disservice through complacency. Ironically, in trying to 'protect' others from difficulty and pain, we stifle their growth. We go from trying to control and avoid uncertainty to creating a future certainty of self-limiting beliefs.

I believe that controversy is the drive behind our social evolution. Our children need us to lead by example. It is our conscious duty to actively explore those daunting ideas which are controversial and with a non-judgement mindset, we seek to evaluate the causes of those controversies - that is, the unbiased honest acceptance of a world that isn't made up of "right and wrong" per se, but contrasting perspectives, values and biases. We can only be part of the solution to world problems if we break the silence that permits them.

Positive Risk-Taking

Positive risks are, well, positive. They are of course 'risky' by nature but they are not risks that will likely lead to real harm or danger. They are risks that when all the evidence is weighed and there are real tangible benefits to be had, you can choose. Choose to either do - or don't do. As Susan Jeffers' amazing seminal book famously states: *"Feel the fear and do it anyway"*. Again, it's all about making a choice.

My mantra is 'I doubt, I do, I conquer'. Of course, I experience doubt, but I no longer hold doubt as a 'bad thing'; instead I actually see it as a reason to go ahead and *do*. This is because experience has shown me that it is better to do a thing and find out something new (even if it is to find out that the thing is not right for you), than to not do it and always wonder. Only if you choose 'do', will you ever conquer anything. Personal growth comes from moving beyond our familiar, our 'safe' and comfortable norms.

Take positive risks, investigate what makes you uncomfortable because it suggests there is something you are avoiding and/or judging. Be curious. *"Feel the fear and do it anyway"*.

In my own experience I have always wanted 'to know rather than always wonder'. That there was no use in regretting what you tried but there would be regrets in not trying. Even if something ventured into was not for me - I reasoned that it was better to try walking in a variety of shoes and to have tested my own boundaries rather than to stay at home and assume. I'd still rather have my mind blown and have to rebuild my understanding of the world, than live in fear of getting a fright.

Here are some examples of my own rather 'iffy' positive risk-taking behaviours and the benefits that came from them.

Snake keeping

As a child, I did unusual things. By ten years old I was the littlest herpetologist in town - I kept snakes. I kept snakes because others maligned them. I wanted to show them fairness - pet-based 'equal opportunities'. Always one for sticking up for the underdog or in this case, the undersnake, I became interested in my ophidian friends when I realised that they were subject to so much prejudice, fear and loathing. I felt a sense of unfairness and so took it upon myself to be their champion. By age 10 I had my first snake, Colin the garter snake and a year or so later I shared my bedroom with a large vivarium containing a breeding pair of corn snakes.

I took one to school for our kind of 'show and tell' day. I delivered a talk on why snakes were awesome and even got to chalk up a 'diagram' of how their forky little tongues worked on the teacher's blackboard. It never occurred to me to be nervous because I was doing good work by sticking up for my lithe little chum. I was EMPOWERED through action that was centred on doing good. There was no fear that kept me back because it was not about me, it was about Colin. I learned there and then, the power of sharing opportunity. I went on to be a fairly confident public speaker and was chair of the school debate team. I still speak publicly today as an advocate of wellbeing practices and as an ally for marginalised communities.

Furthermore, I still take snakes into schools. I have two Royal Pythons (Norman and Delilah) who have been handled by hundreds of primary age children in wellbeing lessons. I engage them as metaphors for 'being differently abled, misunderstood and underestimated' and ignite discussion about 'transitions' - that snakes are a power symbol for healing, and that just as the snake repeatedly sheds its skin, we too go through changes in life where we can emerge stronger every time.

The children often ask: *"Will it bite me?"*

I say: *"Probably not"*

I see many raised eyebrows on little faces. They are perhaps used to adults lying with guarantees of safety but where is the fun or growth in a 'no risk encounter'? I know the snakes well and also how to hold them for everyone's safety, however, being honest that a bit of risk was involved taught respect for risk-taking and, respect for the animal's 'right to bite' as the snake didn't have a choice in taking a risk - (s)he was going to be held by little hands regardless.

The opportunity led to teaching the "3 Cs" of animal handling (Care, Calm and Confidence) which created opportunity for all those children to take a positive risk, consider empathy and grow beyond their fears and assumptions.

Baring All

As an adult, I increasingly notice the spiral of events in my life - not to be confused with going round in circles, loops or mere repetition (see diagram in previous section on comfort zones). In a spiral motion I return back to the same themes, places and people and each time expand my understanding and ability, to help others.

> *"Insanity is doing the same thing over and over again*
> *and expecting different results."*
> **Attributed to Albert Einstein**
> *(although this remains debated, it's a great quote so here it is!)*

Also, it can be seen in my career as a fetish model and in the 'Ministry of Burlesque' mission where I posed for latex designers rather than kids catalogues, and I performed burlesque instead of ballet. I was rejected from the 'norm', and so I created the antidote by challenging those norms. Through this I overcame so much. There is nothing like public nudity to challenge your tolerance to anxiety. You might say I was positive risqué taking.

Thinking back to the time I decided I had to perform my first ever burlesque routine reminded me similarly of the sheer force that Anxiety can wield - for good. Through this one, 3-minute long, totally half-baked comedic dance routine, I achieved so much more than I could possibly have known at the time. To date, I have produced near a thousand burlesque shows, have travelled the world and met many friends. Biggest of all is that in helping to actually create an artistic industry, many people now enjoy real careers in a genre that challenges body, gender and beauty norms, celebrates diversity and offers opportunity for others to grow and believe in themselves. For this I will always be grateful to Anxiety - for showing me the power of *positive risk-taking.*

Scared of the Dark?

Similarly, when I was a paranormal investigator (formally for a research group, the BBC, and private individuals and also for leisure companies running 'ghost hunts'), I enjoyed the risk taking of literally stepping into the dark to confront imagined (or was it real?) spooky phenomena. Watching others challenge and encounter their own fears (and possibly a few entities) was utterly fascinating. The full range of Anxiety's performance repertoire would be on show driving each person to take their individual actions, make choices and interpret what they were experiencing - and what it meant to them. Many left those events, transformed.

So snakes, public nudity and haunted buildings were right for me but may feel a bit extreme for others. So, where to start in positive risk taking?

Either actively do that exciting thing you've been contemplating. Take the risk for an outcome you already want. Or, if you don't want to invest in your *dreams*, investigate your *nightmares* - or at least, something you know that you avoid.

Putting the Ritual in Spirituality

There is often a lot of naysaying around ritual - as though it equates to silly 'un-scientific' superstition and compulsive behaviours such as those negatively associated with OCD. In such instances 'superstitious thinking' is where a person mistakenly attributes their 'bad thoughts' as having a causal association with events in the real world - that they then feel responsible for, (and hence the need to 'neutralise' or counter-act these thoughts with compulsions). E.g. On thinking that their colleague is preventing them from career progress and wishing they would quit and then associating that with a coincidental accident or illness that person endures. It is easy to get muddled up on this one as it is a very loaded word. 'Ritual' is a word loaded with connotations of things that provoke Anxiety for many including negative associations with religious practice such as the go-to collocations of 'ritual sacrifice', 'ritual chanting', 'ritual cleansing' and 'ritual drinking', etc. These all sound a bit extreme and scary to most. Even in the mental health profession, practitioners often talk about ritual and even spirituality by extension, as though they should be discouraged but this is akin to throwing the baby out with the bathwater.

Rituals in their true sense are simply personal practical methods of mentally and emotionally focusing on a desired outcome. Top achieving athletes, performers and businesspeople tend to employ rituals to help them engage in a certain 'winning' mindset. I asked international superhuman Immodesty Blaize for her thoughts on this. As someone with an amazing personal career of being in the spotlight as a burlesque star, style icon, author and mind-body eating coach she is a great example of how ritual empowers. She says: *"Personal ritual is a symbolic and grounding act of support to self, a preparation which honours and brings meaning and care to the task or day ahead. I choose from a variety of processes to suit the occasion, including breathwork, chanting, a series of stretches. It could be in the way I lay out my dressing room, the way I carve out a minute of repose to be still, or the first words I speak out loud when I wake. Ritual banishes superstition or obsessive compulsive action by bringing you into your internal power, rather than giving it away to external placebo like the 'lucky necklace' or 'knock 10 times on wood'. I use personal ritual to channel stage or performance nerves into a positive energy, and to stay calm under pressure, such as live TV or frenetic discombobulating environments. As I travel a lot, the familiarity of ritual is a comfort no matter where in the world I am. It helps reduce anxiety attacks, and I use it as regular self-care practice at home."*

From mantras and mandalas to physical routines and prayers - all of these are perfectly healthy, calming and enjoyable practices. What they all have in common is that they are personally meaningful, repetition-based and actively *practiced*. Think on about how you might enhance a good night's sleep with an evening self-care ritual - this could be affirmations in the mirror, a hot drink and some lovely facial cleansing products. It's no different from when we encourage children to adopt and practice a bed-time *routine*. Such a routine often involves warm milk, a bath and the adorning of special clothes (dinosaur PJs). So, this is usually a combination of ritual cleansing and imbibing. It's a great example of the power of language - and what we choose to experience.

The key lesson here is of choosing how to program your mind-body connection. That conscious rituals create unconscious habits. Regularly performed, positive personal rituals - with carefully crafted actions and language, meaning and intention - will help you to wire (and re-wire) your mind and body for healthy everyday thinking and behavioural habits. Such conscious rituals will help you to focus your attention on creating the life you want, rather than maintaining the anxious cycle of intrusive thoughts and unhelpful compulsions that keep you down.

Fall in love with what you hate

Love and hate are two sides of the same coin. Have you ever noticed how quickly something you love can become something you can't stand to be around? Or vice versa? Enthusiasts of olives often say they can remember when they used to hate them and now act as some kind of culinary Tony Robbins on a mission to transform tastebuds. On perhaps a higher level, romance is made up of this dichotomy of love and hate. So the same with the fear-excitement aspect of Anxiety.

Go to art galleries and look at the stuff you don't like - what is it that you don't like? Ask yourself why? How is this challenging to you? Even if you are dismissing it as 'crap a five year old could do' Isn't the fact that it's challenging you the whole point? Regardless? Touché artists... touché.

Watch a film or read a book that you've been actively avoiding. Now I don't mean go do something you feel is a waste of your time, things where there is no risk and no reward (e.g. maybe you avoid pairing your socks or watching a sport you find uninteresting). Be sure to choose something that you know holds merit or value for others whom you respect and crucially, that it feels risky for you personally - that you might be challenged by it. Remember, there is something in your avoidance behaviour that is screaming out to be discovered!

If you find you spend a LOT of time on social media browsing and looking, you could consider that this is procrastinating from your goal of self-development. If so, be sure to remember that action is needed.

You need to *do* something that is meaningful to you - all the time spent reposting and 'sharing if you agree' is a lot less helpful than the *action* and it is allowing you *avoid* the task.

The ironic gift of Anxiety

Concluding this part of the book, I want you to learn to notice the ironies in each experience you have - and laugh at yourself (e.g. worrying about a test you might not even take, worrying about causing a car accident when you can't even drive, taking hair straighteners on a road trip to avert Anxiety - and so on).

All that time you have spent in elaborate hypothetical realities, time travelling to anywhere but the present moment, combined with the emotional rollercoasters, the physical dizzying highs and shivering lows, the going over and over and over all the potential ifs and buts rehearsing the many possible outcomes in your head - especially the worst ones imaginable.

How many of these are familiar to you?

Planning (alternative road routes because there might be an accident or roadblock or an emergency situation).

Mental Rehearsal (to avoid flupping up, embarrassing yourself or in case of an emergency situation).

Emotional Intelligence (reading the situations of others).

Empathic sensitivity (overwhelmed by interacting with others who probably see your stress and tears as emotional 'weakness').

Use of ritual (superstitious mumbo-jumbo that takes up all your time because you need it to feel 'right' before you can do X,Y or Z).

Mind-body connectivity (overwhelmed by noticing changes in the body that suggest illness and death... or maybe just impending mortal embarrassment).

Creative thinking (just can't stop thinking about all the terrible that might happen and/or the many interpretations of what they meant when they said...).

Imagination (All the terrible horrendous detail in full HD with surround-sound and... the astronomical consequences that will unfold).

I bet you 10p you can add to this list!

But what If...

You are actually sitting on a goldmine of 'super-psyche skills'? It's just that you are erm, doing it in the wrong direction?

Considering all that we have looked at so far, ponder upon how your past uncomfortable experiences actually benefit the present and future you - where you can flip them from being a weight at your front to a force at your back. Think of those mental, physical and emotional habits as hard-core training for what can now become an immense personal development journey. Anxiety might (until now) have been your curse - but you are the hero of this story and choosing to move forward as the holistic superhuman you are, is everyone's blessing.

You are likely to have expert skills in some or even all of these, it's just that you currently use them for worry, illness and exhaustion - rather than growth:

Planning (clarity of direction, strategist).

Mental Rehearsal (enhances memory and performance focus).

Emotional Intelligence (reading and responding well to the situations of others, a huge indicator of success in life btw...).

Empathic sensitivity (emotional connectivity).

Use of ritual (for highly focused visualization, intention and goal setting).

Mind-body connectivity (self-awareness, healing, aligned action).

Creative thinking (innovation, problem solving).

Imagination (you can reach for and grasp the stars - and way beyond, limitless potential).

Until now, you've only been focused on the negative direction of these skills, probably because you have never even regarded them as skills. Do you know who would chew their own arms off for this set of skills? Everyone. Everyone who wants to take charge of manifesting their best and most fulfilling lives - these skills are the very skills and habits that are purposefully cultivated by the most successful life coaches, entrepreneurs, athletes, performing artists, scientists, politicians and social leaders. You are sitting on them and yet they make you uncomfortable. It's time to realise you need to move your butt off the awkward assumptions and negative self-limiting beliefs and instead, look forward in the right direction, the direction of growth.

Look back over those skills and consider what employer, lover, community, business, audience... would NOT want those in you?

Next time you suspect a vicious cycle may be driving you, picture the cartoon below and remind yourself you have *choice*. Get off and take a taxi, or a luxury limo - or even better go for a mindful walk.

Think about your thoughts, physical sensations, behaviours and emotions. What are they telling you about who you are now? What are those core values and what change do you want to be and see in life? What is the potential within you and in the world around you? Now that you are your own ally, what will you do differently?

Of course, you are not on your own.

What if.... The Universe itself also has your back?

It does.

CHAPTER TWO

EVERYTHING IS BECAUSE IT ISN'T

Freethinkers understand there is a difference in knowing *how* to think over *what* to think. It's too easy and to be frank, lazy, to just accept what someone else tells you - even if you 'feel' it's true. Remember, that could be emotional reasoning at play. The feelings tell us about how *we respond* to things - not an inherent truth about anything 'out there'. Our emotions are the biggest indicator of where we need to turn our attention and what to address for our own growth.

Since the aim of this book is to encourage you to transcend *beyond* Anxiety, using what it teaches you from within your inner world (your 'microcosm') can now be applied way beyond - to the bigger scale Universe of all things (Macrocosm). So, with this in mind let's have a ponder upon some important concepts for thinking - thinking in the wider, bigger, even cosmic-scale sense.

Fancy words for straight thinking

If you want to be able to use your thinking mind as a free thinker, this is where our philosophical buddies *Epistemology* and *Ontology* come in - because they are the pillars of strength in realising how and what we *really* think. It's easy to be put off by ideas that sound overly serious, academic or philosophical, but they actually sound far fancier as words than they are (and it is ok to be fancy anyway).

Ontology - basically, it's 'thinking about the nature of being' - how we understand, categorise and contextualise things, e.g. "why is a horse not a duck? What are the duckly traits that define duckiness? And so on... *Ontology* is how we define and categorise our world. It's asking 'what IS this? And, what is it NOT?'

Epistemology - basically its 'thinking about thinking' - how we think and what it means to talk about knowledge, e.g. "How do I know that I know things? What does it mean to *believe* something... rather than *know* it? What is a fact anyway?"

It's all 'very meta'! Yes, it is rather. In fact, it is related to understanding *metaphysics* and *non-duality*, but we will come to the relevance of these important concepts later. Again, they can sound rather intimidating and science-y but they are not as complicated as they seem. In fact, once you start to apply them to your experiences of Anxiety and beyond, you will see just how cheerfully simple and wonderful it all is. Oh! How ironic!

So... am I a potato?

What is a potato? What *is* a potato waffle (and *is* it still potato)? How many 'facts' about potatoes makes a true example of one?

What if we make chips out of one? Is it no longer *a* potato yet *made of* potato? At what point does it become French fries?

What about a horse? How do we define what makes it a horse? 4 legs? Mane? Goes clip-clop? Doesn't perform magic from its face? What if it swapped its flowing locks for a cool 80s wet-perm? What if it was born with only 3 legs? What is the essential intrinsic thing that defines it? Why is it not also a lion?

Epistemology helps us to further consider the differences between what might be a fact, a belief and also how we 'justify' things. We often feel anxious because we believe things to be a threat which are factually untrue. Yet we believe them to be a threat. We might even justify the threat through the cognitive distortions.

By starting to notice *how* we are thinking, we can start to unpick and untangle our fears to reveal the possibility that we don't need to be afraid - because there are no 'facts' to rely on, instead just a belief about a threat.

Think about those things that trigger Anxiety for you. How about snakes? What are the defining aspects that make up a snake? By teasing out the elements of 'is-ness', there comes a point when you have a collection of 'qualities' rather than the overall snake.

At what point does it cease to be an overall thing of fear? When you take out the venom? When you take out the body shape? What about what you actually know versus what you believe about them? How reliable is your information?

Can you work out which element or elements is/are causing you fear? If it's venom, does it matter that most snakes are non-venomous? Is your fear then also triggered by other venomous or poisonous species? What about toxic plants?

"The only true wisdom is in knowing you know nothing."
Socrates

And his equally famous student then said...

"I am the wisest man alive, for I know one thing,
and that is that I know nothing."
Plato

EXAMPLE:

I experience 'trypophobia' - loosely speaking it's the fear of seeing clusters of little holes or spheres - like in those horrid seedpods (bleh! *shudders*). You often find these creepy holey flups lurking in potpourri (*shudders again*).

Similarly, it's often triggered by some kinds of fossilised coral or sponges. For many other trypophobics it is in a visual comparison to tiny insect or arachnid egg clusters ready to hatch, or in not knowing what might be hiding inside the 'holes'. It's currently not recognised by clinical diagnostic tools as a 'phobia' per se as it's more a deep sense of revulsion rather than fear, however, this definition of phobia remains debated but, in any case, it provokes immense Anxiety and it's a surprisingly common phenomenon.

However, to put the ontological point on this - I'm totally fine with similar clusters that aren't 'holes' per se e.g. bubbles (I love bubbles) but I definitely do not love giant sunflowers of which I feel a sudden sense of suspicion. Those creepy badgers make me shudder - although little sunflowers are ok, in fact pretty and mathematically reassuring somehow. Unpack this for me and write me an answer on a postcard please... Absurd, right?

In terms of epistemology, am I even thinking about this? Am I assuming I know something factual that others don't? Am I drawing on the emotion of a childhood memory when I saw a worm peek out of a hole in an apple? Point is, I need to consider what I think I know, what I believe and how I'm justifying those beliefs.

Try also applying this understanding to *situations* that provoke worry for you. Where? What's going on? Whittle it down and see what the essential qualities or components are and, what you can drop from the assumption. Be as specific as you can be. You'll find you are left with very little to hold on to, if anything - and in the words of a certain Elsa - you could maybe even "Let it Go..."

This 'is-ness' of things is at the heart of philosophical thinking and taking it further, it helps us to appreciate that what we 'are' is just as meaningful to contemplate as what we *are not*. If we can think in detachment - without emotional judgement that one thing or state is better or preferable than the other - we see that *is* and *isn't* are actually contrasting labels for experiencing the same thing - just like 'heads and tails', 'light and dark', '1 and 0'.

We probably are potatoes just as much as we aren't. Have you ever compared the chemical and genetic make-up of potatoes and people, or bananas and people for that matter? What *is* same? What *is* shared? What *is* the difference? Perhaps in sharing how we are different; we are also rather ironically sharing sameness - sameness of *is* and sameness of *is not*.

Let's think of the 'is-ness' of a dog called Boris. what makes him a dog? What makes him Boris the dog (is it his anatomy, genealogy, behaviour, name, breed label?). Essentially Boris is actually made up mainly of space (just like the rest of us), lots of space between each Boris building atom. So, if we were to measure Boris, where do the boundaries of Boris lie? Tip of his nose? End of his fur? The spaces between the fur? What if he went bald? Where does Boris stop being Boris and become the environment around him? Or, Stacey Biteycheex the flea that hides burrowed in his skin? What of the chemical boundary between Boris's bladder and the pot plant he likes to wee on when no one is looking?

What is plant, what is dog, what is chemistry, what is space? What do you know to be true about doggo biology? What do you believe or just assume is true? When he eats and digests his dinner, at what point does the food stop being the food and become part of Boris? What about when he poops it out on the lawn?

What if... you took this further. Imagine you are petting Boris. Where does the dog end and you begin? How do you define the difference or separation? It's all relative and based on personal observation. There are no defined boundaries or separation beyond perception. There is a constant flow of exchange and transmutation occurring in you, with you and through you.

What I'm getting at here is the interconnectedness of Life, The Universe and Everything. That boundaries and definitions are ultimately illusory, impermanent, subjective and well - non-existent beyond perception.

Two side of the same coins, two ends of the same spectrum... there is no definitive 'this or that' there is ALL the possibility to be had. This is why when our anxious minds jump to a negative conclusion or assumption, we must also give credit equally to the other opposite side of the coin or spectrum as being just as plausible... Here in the proverbial 'gap' between perceived this or that we find a whole universe of potential to *choose* from instead. Here everything in between the extremes becomes far more realistic.

Maybe instead of thinking 'I will definitely fail this test', you might consider the opposite 'I will definitely ace this test' as being an equally valid possibility. What about all the options in between like not even going to the test, taking a different test, the test being cancelled, not passing and finding a much, much better course instead, passing it with flying psychedelic colours and hating the resulting job you get and choosing something else anyway?

The 'Gap'

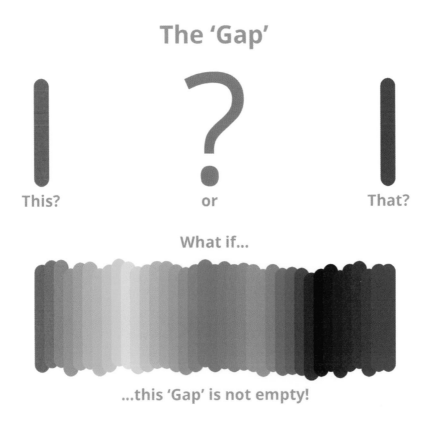

This?   or   That?

What if...

...this 'Gap' is not empty!

What does it really matter? You always have a spectrum of choices.

When experiencing something like fear why not also consider growth? In sadness you can also consider joy. In failure you might look to success... and so on. Here is a list of apparent 'opposites' that all contain an enormous spectrum of likelihood:

Fear - Growth

Sadness - Joy

Hate - Love

Doubt - Faith

Impossible - Guaranteed

Decay - Life

Failure - Success

Exhaustion - Creativity

Dark - Light

Denial - Acceptance

Resentment - Forgiveness

Apathy - Hope

You might debate some of these (debate is healthy and such concepts are personal anyway) and I'm sure that you can add to this list too. Another 10p for your bag of two-sided coins.

Maybe instead of assuming you will accidentally burn down your village, perhaps instead you might consider that maybe you could save your village in an equally elaborate story? What of all the other options in between? What if absolutely nothing ever happened in your village?

In fact, if we want to get all multi-dimensional and add in other worries as factors, we can create elaborate scenarios for great things - in place of disasters. This is how you turn nightmares into dreams.

A true sceptic is a child-like enquirer

Similarly, the idea (and often media trend) of *scepticism* offers up a load of hidden traps. To be sceptical is originally to remain open-minded, **non-judgemental**, to lean with the weight of evidence and not be swayed by emotional or biased reasoning.

Being sceptical is about being honest - honest with yourself in the moment and also perhaps, honest about not really having a clue.

Scepticism originally comes from the word 'skeptikos', meaning 'seeker' but more recently it has come as an often belief-loaded statement of negation.

The trend has led many (including in the scientific community) to confusingly and erroneously equate an absence of belief, with belief statements of denial (to say that something 'definitely does not exist', which is a belief). Often, media loving scientists are very quick and loud in the rubbishing of other people's beliefs - but cite their own beliefs as though they are fundamentally true. The nuts of the mistake is this:

"There is no God... because I don't believe in one... because I haven't seen the evidence... because I'm only looking at certain styles of evidence... because I believe in one style of evidence... because...)"

You see? A nuanced but important difference.

Modern scepticism, in my view is a watered-down version of Pyrrhonism (named after its founding thinker Pyrrho of Elis (c.360 - c.270 BCE) whose teachings were written by Sextus Empiricus.

Often confused with scepticism, it differs in a subtle but crucial way.

Expert scholar Adrian Kuzminski explains this difference perfectly in the opening of his book, *Phyrrhonism: How the Ancient Greeks Reinvented Buddhism*. He says: *"Unlike sceptics, who believe 'there are no true beliefs', Pyrrhonists suspend judgement about all beliefs including the belief that there are no true beliefs."*

That is, no beliefs - pro or con - can be held beyond that which is 'self-evident'.

For example, where they do accept beliefs in 'self-evident' matter such as where a person scratches their nose, it's acceptable to believe there was an itch. In contrast, for example, believing in a particular deity's responsibility for a good harvest (even when it's cyclical or repeating) is not self-evident - it cannot be confirmed or disconfirmed. So, why entangle yourself with the potential torment of expectations dashed and eternal uncertainty?

Very similar to a Buddhist approach, Pyrrhonism asserts that there is no way to know anything to be true or not and so by throwing out notions of beliefs to anything that is not self-evident (like the itchy nose), they avoid the unnecessary Anxiety that is created by the uncertainty.

"If you can solve the problem, then what is the need of worrying?
If you cannot solve it, then what is the use of worrying?"
Shantideva

Furthermore, as anxious experiences take hold in our lives, we can think of the lesson here: that if our physical sensations, thoughts and feelings are the *self-evident* involuntary events that we do indeed experience, that's all we've got! We cannot go beyond noticing them to reach any kind of *non-evident* belief *about* them. By accepting the experiences for what they are (physical and mental events) and dropping any attachment to what they 'mean' we avoid the vicious cycle of negative beliefs and tangle of anxious worry.

This is a *practice* and the goal is indeed a therapeutic one - to achieve freedom from anxiety, tranquillity - ataraxia. In Pyrrhonism, the thinker would always throw out any sense of acceptance of their own conclusion so as not to fall into the trap of mistaking an unhelpful belief for a false fact. Pyrrhonists live according to what is really, actually occurring in real time and not according to hypothetical ideas. They would truly remain open-minded and unburdened in their hearts - enlightened, you might say.

As in all forms of enquiry, in science, there is often a lot of 'position holding' going on, even when ideally a sense of neutrality would be beneficial. This essentially means that when someone is 'holding a position' they are making a statement of belief - and it often looks like:

"X does exist."

or

"X does *not* exist."

To be sceptical about something means that if you do hold a position on a given hypothesis, it is done so according to the weight of evidence - and should be open to change if that evidence should change. So, a sceptic might accurately say that based on evidence, they do not believe that god or ghosts or ESP or aliens exist (because they have not been convinced by a 'weight of evidence' that they do). But they cannot make outright claims of non-existence because they similarly have not had it *dis*-proved to them.

However, equally they are *not* saying 'there is *no* god/ghosts *don't* exist' and so on. This is because to state that something *does NOT exist* is in fact taking a position or holding a *belief* - just as the same as it is to state that something *does* exist.

Positions of belief:

"There is a X, Y or Z" (Says who? Prove it!) / "There is not a X, Y or Z" (Says who? Prove it!)

Unfortunately, the trend for scepticism is (ironically) emotionally driven - it holds a lot of social and peer acceptance to maintain a status quo of thinking style, along with the current peculiar 'norm' of throwing out much of human experience, in favour of *only* the empirical data extracted from experiments.

Empirical data is of course crucial in the underpinning of so much science and development - in areas like medicine (chemistry, physics, biology all rolled into one) where being able to predict outcomes is essential.

But there are other forms of information too and certain quests for understanding can't rely on a singular methodology to the exclusion of all others; this is because we are often asking different kinds of questions and making different kinds of predictions.

For example, many self-penned sceptics love to cite 'logic' as though it is the one 'true' method of thinking. Logic is great for solving *logical* problems, like those 'if-or-and-then' stuff in computer programming and electronics.

Yet logic can't tell you what your favourite colour is or why, it can't explain the meaning of life, it can't answer your existential BIG Questions, it certainly can't tell you what your cat fancies for tea. Not even cat logic can do that. Yet so many 'believe' (ironic, right?) that logic can answer everything.

Serious thinkers, of all genres of thought styles, striving to be without the bias of their cultural paradigm (a collective set of principles or assumptions), are tending increasingly toward mystical or spiritual outlooks to resolve the pervading 'big questions'- because ideas of nonduality become needed and arguments about 'rightness' and 'wrongness' become rather redundant.

"If you believe what you like in the Gospel, and reject what you don't like, it is not the Gospel you believe, but yourself."

St. Augustine

Beware of the dog(ma)

From pulpit to soapbox to peer-reviewed journals, dogma is everywhere. Dogma takes the form of a set of principles that are incontrovertible. As a fourteen year old I argued with my then minister over misogyny and homophobia in Leviticus, and was erm... kicked out of church. As a young adult, I debated with my academic mentors over the validity of 'anomalous experience' and was laughed at. We all experience dogma and it can be very subtle. The dogma of our peer groups and social circles might dictate what is correct or incorrect to wear, say, do - and in the workplace, outdated 'policies and procedures' are often the broken backbone of the many prejudicial 'isms we face.

Thinking back on my own encounters of anomalous or 'paranormal' phenomena, what I or anyone else might have experienced is relative, personal, and entirely subjective.

So, who is anyone else - whose brain was not processing the experience - to declare it irrelevant, mistaken or even fictitious? On what authority? Surely, not one of an assumed personal sense of correctness? That would sound suspiciously unscientific, dogmatic. It would sound a lot like assumption and closed-mindedness.

Besides, people report phenomena as it's their own personal experience in real time influenced by all sorts of infinite things and relayed in our limited language. They are not stating newly decreed existential facts about the nature of universe.

"I saw a ghost!"

...is likely to be equivalent to

"I've just had an experience that can be best described in the words 'I saw a ghost!' but I'm shocked as I don't know what to think about the nature of reality now and I need to express this conundrum as my brain might explode."

...and there often someone who says "Well, as a sceptic *I* think... You are clearly mistaken/ill/lying." feeling the need to defend the position despite not being involved nor asked. I should point out here that the term 'scepticism' is often misused and misrepresented as 'naysaying'.

In claiming not only to have a superior and correct opinion about the existence (or non-existence) of paranormality, they also appear to ironically assume they have magical psychic insight into what was really going on in someone else's brain, mind and body despite not being involved.

Suspending (dis)belief where yours is challenged is really important. We don't all have to believe the same thing - because reality is a personal experience. What we do share is the discussion.

What often happens in fact is that when someone is keen to dismiss and rubbish something - even though they have been not involved in it themselves - they do so because they feel that their core values and deeply held beliefs have been challenged in a deep way.

Here, in this 'intervention' they mistake their emotional position for intellectual rigour. The ego can help us do that when we feel challenged. When someone claims scepticism from a fast-held belief position, we call this *dogma* and it is rife in academia, research, and scientific media. Ironic, considering the millennia of persecution, frustration and sabotage experienced by scientists at the hands of the church. Fools are innocent in their ignorance, fool-hardy and openly paving the way for a journey of learning but dogmatists are ironic fools that won't budge, they can't learn because they are closed, blindly stuck in their awkward positions always wondering why other people's experiences upset them so.

The role of The Ego in Anxiety and in un-consciousness

The Ego is an illusion - it is who you think you are, comprised of all sorts of things (from haircut, gender, race, occupation, blood type, GSOH...to the media you subscribe to and the news you believe). You are none of these things. Your true nature is hidden behind the many masks that ego wears. You have to look in the mirror and see past your own ego - to see past the Anxiety that it manifests.

Your ego does not want you to see that it is there - because if you don't know it's there, you won't challenge it. This is self-preservation of identity. If your identity is challenged, all else might unravel.

Perhaps, somewhat existentially, you are anxious about getting to know yourself - worried about who (or what) might be lurking 'in there' - but this is just the ego tricking you as it doesn't want any weak spots exposed. Its main role is to defend itself from dissolution.

Anxiety also sneakingly operates on an egoic level - it's always trying to defend its position of control by assuming ultimate correctness. By dropping ego, we can better perceive who we are - without personal emotional bias, cultural influences, peer trends, beliefs and personality trait. Self-esteem can be tricky as it often manifests as perceived polarities which create anxious thoughts and behaviours about the self in the forms of self-loathing or vanity. Both being unappealing concepts that we would avoid acknowledging. In fact, I'd say these two traits aren't opposites, they are one in the same egoic self-defence. Two ends of the same spectrum. Two sides of the same coin. With self-love and self-acceptance landing in the middle.

Instead of letting Anxiety be a trick to keep you egocentric, see it as motivation and an opportunity to employ self-reflection - where you have something tangible to work on. Many people seeking enlightenment or self-development would kill to have something to wrestle with. It's like being in that mental gym, you use the weights to build strength, not to hold you down. Think if it like this... The very process of finding enlightenment is hidden in the word itself... en-lighten-ment - literally to lighten your load, give up the burden you bear.

Being present in the moment, the 'now' instead of the past or potential future, disarms the ego and therefore Anxiety stands down.

Life is lived through a lens or two, or three or...

From examining bacteria on a Petri dish through a microscope to watching the proverbial fat lady sing through those little opera glasses, all culture is viewed, assessed and even judged through a selection of lenses.

"The unexamined life is not worth living."
Socrates

We all experience Anxiety idiosyncratically. It's *personal.* Although we share common thoughts, feelings, sensations and behaviours, the personal anxious experience is born out of our many biases - those personal and cultural 'lenses' through which we have viewed and continue to view Life, The Universe and Everything. Psychologists often refer to these collective lenses as 'schemas', meaning a 'scheme' or pattern of thinking that organises our thoughts and actions in a kind of framework, one that then predicts future understanding and doing.

When we have problems with our vision we get an eye test. We go to an optician who then experiments with various lenses to correct our vision bringing it to an optimal place usually with a personal prescription for specs or contact lenses. Such lenses are 'correcting' a deficit.

Similarly, when we watch films or look at glossy magazine images, we view 'beauty' as presented through a system of lenses, adjusted for optimal presentation. From soft focus cameras and HD screens we are presented with a *version* of what was really on set. Such lenses are presenting an ideal.

But what of the many conceptual lenses that we cannot see? Our biases?

Think of our life journey as though we exist in a hot house of perception. We start out as little seeds full of potential, we are planted in the soil, then seek nourishment and light to grow and bloom. Our nourishment depends on many factors and our growth is the outcome of what we are given and how much light we are exposed to. We might grow toward the light and blossom,

or, we might not. Let's explore the greenhouse effect of intense lens wearing.

So many lenses are granted *at birth* as either *predispositions* of our DNA and the womb environment in which we form. We then consider the *circumstances* that we are born *in to*. Then we look at those *influences* over time that we *grow*.

Granted by Nature at Birth

For example, at birth we generally find ourselves granted a set of lenses according to the following: gender (an iffy subject in itself), ethnicity, our genetically determined traits and quirks. We may be born differently abled or transgender, neurologically diverse or so many other interesting things, but it's very likely that such diversity goes unrecognised... until we start to struggle in a world designed for typicality and/or perhaps we dare to stand out as a spokesperson for change in a 'normal' society.

Granted by Circumstance at Birth

Then we consider what we are born in to and the lenses we are immediately given: the era of birth, geography, social status and wealth of your family and community, popular trends at the time. These are great examples of factors that determine wildly varying social norms (can you imagine how different life would be if you were born in the 1700s?).

Acquired on our Journeys

Thirdly, there are those biases acquired as we grow and learn how to interact with (and how to react to) the world: health, education, social circles, romance, careers, politics, chance events, finances and media course the many multi-faceted layers of parental influence and their inherited experiential legacies.

Whatever earworm was playing at No 1 in the charts may have a lot to answer for, but more seriously, trends on public health, politics, education, domestic cleaning, diets, fashion, medical and psychological theories are all HUGE influences - even where you might never have directly interacted with them because they are the cultural weather outside. They are the basic 'stock' that all your nourishment is cooked in.

Lenses may in some cases enhance our viewing like a telescope, a microscope, a pair of spectacles for our myopia, a magnifying glass to go with our deerstalkers when there is a mystery afoot - who doesn't enjoy a lovely monocle for inspecting vintage

Sherry bottles in the 1920s, what! what! But these are lenses we purposefully acquire because of an identified need. Where lenses generate difficulty is in the very obvious challenge of sharing perspective or outlook with others. Furthermore - we don't tend to notice that we are even wearing them!

Consider: How easy is it for two people from the same neighbourhood to see eye to eye, compared with two people with very different sets of lenses to see eye to eye? What about a mixed group of 20 children in a classroom? How about 50,000 people in a city? How about the population of the world?

On a personal level, the inability to see anything clearly leads to two main problems:

1. lack of personal clarity about what we see and believe.

2. assumptions about what others see and believe.

This two-factor combination often leads to discord, argument, suspicion, mistrust and prejudice between individuals, communities, countries and cultures.

Our memories are creative acts

Consider too that our experience of time affects our biases.

Psychologists have shown that eyewitness testimony in court to be often unreliable. Our memories are snapshots of experience as seen through multiple lenses, with a lot of 'scene missing' moments. We actually construct much of our memories *as we are remembering them!* Ironic, right? So, our memories are only ever as accurate as the last time we retrieved the memory meaning that upon each retrieval, the memory is slightly altered. Nostalgia is a special fluffy version of life as viewed through rose-tinted retro-spectacles, it is a lens showing us a past that never happened.

Knickers in a twist? It's cool... We are all cross-dressers.

It is worth taking a moment to consider gender in specific.

Gender is one of those interesting constructs that are generally oversimplified as a 'this or that' scenario. The reality is that each of us contains both masculine and feminine qualities, energies and abilities. The whole symbolism of marriage is one of the *Union* of genders - of masculine and feminine coming together as the Universe is itself both identities.

Marriage (often referred to as 'union' by clerics) is an ancient magical act of divine gratitude that honours the merging of the masculine and feminine - but this is not about 'a man and a woman' because each human possesses both qualities.

Many cultures find the notion of a 'this or that' ideology on gender to be absurd. For example, India has a 'third gender' that to most Westerners seems like a blend of masculinity and femininity expressed in the individual. Native American tribes hold four possible gender identities as sacred where the physical body and the inherent spirit of the person make up one of the following four identities: Masculine/Masculine, Feminine/Feminine, Masculine/Feminine and Feminine/Masculine. Such people would not label themselves as transgender or gender non-binary (nor any of our contemporary notions of understanding blended gender as though it is a new thing). These concepts are simply not needed to 'explain' anything and in many ways, miss the point of the divine union within the individual. The notion of masculine OR feminine is an oversimplification.

It's in our choice of expression that we then start to label identity as either 'this or that' but in truth we are all, both. We are all made up of male and female DNA because we are made of both our mothers AND fathers - not one 'or' the other. Considering the Big(ish) Question of 'why do men have nipples?'

We can see that we are all androgynous in the womb up until certain hormone changes occur, often change actually directed by the mother's body. Whatever sex we are then born as according to our genitals is as arbitrary as what eye colour we have. Yet oddly in society we don't have too much of an issue with one earlobe shape commanding a higher wage over another as we do with perceived gender or skin colour.

Since gender politics is such an extraordinary source of Anxiety, it's important to realise that we can drop this 'polarising' of people and instead appreciate the power of being a society of united beings, all made of both energies. Energies we can harness and express.

The ideas of what a girl, boy, woman, man 'should' wear or do in life is more or less just marketing strategies to sell us stuff, and political strategies to win votes. Women's hygiene products are packaged in pink and cost more. Boys used to wear pink (seen as visceral) and girls used to wear blue (seen as calming) until a 20th century re-brand. All toys were sold together until a sales team realised that if they had separate girls and boys sections they could double their profits.

Being cisgender, transgender or non-binary are identities that we either are lumped with at birth and stick to - or choose - meaning identities are something we *create*.

They aren't really who we are at the true 'being' level, they are our self-*expression*.

EXERCISE - *Name your own lenses!*

Closer to home and the heart, romance and relationships are also subject to this issue.

Often in a topsy-turvy way. Have you ever lusted after some absolute god or goddess of a human being only to be heartbroken when they were not as kind or as smart or as loving as you expected? We are often attracted to our biased ideals of others - not the reality. Expectations are the root cause of disappointment and it's not just 'beer goggles' at play, it's a heady cocktail of desire, need, fantasy and self-esteem goggles.

Where couples row, there is often a similar 'lens bias' issue. Sometimes one partner cannot see where a certain 'line' is over a sensitive topic (you ever had that other-half who just didn't know when to stop making jokes and you just can't see what's so damn funny?).

Sometimes it's a gender-role clash of expectations of duty and no-one can see that boundaries need to be established - or worse, one party refuses to see them or smashes right through them.

Personal boundaries and fantasy viewing are also absolutely key in other relationship dynamics - including friendships, relationships with parents or siblings, colleagues and your boss. This why so many of us have animal companions! Animal companions don't bother with any of that lens stuff, they don't judge. And that's what this is all about - *JUDGEMENT*.

Despite their frequent facial expressions of minor incredulity, cat's don't actually criticise, budgies don't judge us (despite their cages) and dogs don't damn anyone (except maybe the postman).

EXERCISE - Lens Laboratory!

Think of someone you know only a little well. Could maybe be a reclusive neighbour, that older lady you see at the same time in the gym every Wednesday, that guy who walks his dog at midnight or the new work colleague who always wears Crocs even in snow. Write down their name and, as far as you can without judgement... begin to list the lenses you think they possess.

a) Can you name them?

b) How many are there?

c) How many more do you think are missing from your list?

d) What would this person likely do with a surprise win of £1,000?

e) Ponder upon just how many assumptions you make and which lenses you call in to action over others.

Now consider that you are viewing all this through your own set of lenses and think again about that £1,000. Are you more or less confident about your assumptions?

So, what do we all do about these chuffing lenses?

Well the IFFY approach is to say "Hey, I see you (but I don't). You see me too (but you actually don't)".

Where those tell-tale emotions start to occur (yep, those Anxiety feelings of racing heart, sick stomach, anger, tension and so on) you can be alerted to that inner guru telling you to stop and think. Drop the vision you are holding because it's total BS.

Instead, to achieve a practical moment of peaceful communication over pointless contest, we need to simply accept the biases of others as OK and also your own biases as OK, but something you can at least to some degree, DROP.

This is not a point of weakness or submission to the view of another, it's a position of power and clarity because you are no longer being controlled by ego or motivated by the bloody fight or flight response. You are dropping lenses that narrow and obscure, thus creating a greater perceptual field for you to stand strong in. You are also creating and holding space for the other person to grow too. Instead of battle lines, it results in the opportunity for negotiation of common ground.

Humanity holds so many lenses of judgement that it's amazing we haven't caught fire. On the other hand, if we were to lose the judginess and become aware of their influence, that is, what it looks like to have and not have them, to hold ALL versions in our understanding, then instead of fire we could create eternal rainbows in an infinity of prisms.

What does this mean (but not mean)? Let's look at it on a larger scale. Let's magnify and upscale our thinking.

Changing Minds, Paradigms

Singing from the same hymn sheet, often in Latin, science and spirituality (or religion, loosely speaking) are singing the same song but to different tunes. Both religious and scientific outlooks are frameworks of understanding. They are giant cultural *lenses*, that occur in and shape the output of different industries such as business, academia and the arts. They are also frameworks for how we address the big questions. They are methods of perception and so, despite contrary appearances, they are not as mutually exclusive as they seem nor are they even contradictory. Sometimes a methodology such as science puts its trust in a primarily mental realm of observable, measurable events and effects. Others of a spiritual nature rely more on a kind of 'felt' experience, and some like a mix of the two. These create overall 'trends' in thinking style and generally outline 'what to assume'. These trends are generally known as *paradigms* thanks to the ground-breaking work of Thomas Kuhn in his 1962 book *The Structure of Scientific Revolutions*.

A paradigm is where there is a kind of unofficial collective agreement that certain underpinning fundamentals are 'true', and as different methodologies and discoveries inform one another, paradigms can *shift* - that is, they can change *the nature of* thinking and believing, across eras of time and geography of space.

Examples of paradigm shifts are when collectively, the thinkers, teachers and investigators of a particular culture agree (or perhaps unconsciously collude) and go from one set of underpinning principles to another. E.g. where the Earth went from being the stoic centre of the cosmos to its rightful place chugging its way around the Sun. Similarly, despite the ancient Greeks already figuring it out, for eons it was held that the Earth was flat until observations of ships 'sinking' into the horizon suggested a rather more spherical countenance. On the religious side of life, in the West we have shifted from dark concepts of inherent sin, hell and damnation to rather brighter outlooks of spirituality, love and acceptance. Not because there has been a shift from any particular religion being wrong or right per se, but because so many have taken off old ill-fitting, broken specs held together with a finger-plaster and instead tried on a healthier new prescription of multi-perspective varifocal, reaction-light lenses that also include scientific ideas as well as spiritual ones.

"A new scientific truth does not triumph by convincing its opponents and making them see the light, but rather because its opponents eventually die, and a new generation grows up that is familiar with it."
Max Planck

In more modern science, there is also a gradual shift away from the Newtonian 'materialist' model (a universe of 'us people who experience the world and its stuff - and the stuff out there in the world') to one of nonduality (we are all 'one') or, the medical model of human experience where for example it was assumed that 'consciousness is an accidental by-product of the biological brain' but now there is growing evidence for a untethered consciousness - one that exists and experiences beyond the activity of a physical brain - is persuading a change of heart (and mind, boom-boom). So, in a weird kind of way science is really rather spiritual, and maybe religions are actually kinds of spiritual science? Maybe?

Remember our pals *Epistemology* and *Ontology*? Well, we are coming full circle back to these guys. Only again it's not a circle, it's an upward spiral because when we revisit the same things but with expanded perception, we aren't going in a loop - we are creating a growing spiral. I can't repeat this sentiment enough... it's like I'm on loop (heh).

Just as feeling something to be true and thinking it to be true can both lead to a sense of belief, how do we ever truly 'know' anything?

Imagine you are a thread in an intricately woven tapestry. Look around you and know what it is to be fully woven into and immersed in the work. But then imagine you are plucked out and held aloft to see the 'bigger picture'. Which perspective or experience is better? Is there a 'better' or just 'different'?

We only truly appreciate something when we are fully immersed in it - yet at the same time to truly perceive it all, we would also need to be totally outside of it. Confused? Me too. That's ok, confusion is often the emotional state of frustration that results from a need to hold this OR that idea as though ideas are mutually exclusive. Instead we can take it all on board.

Rather than those cognitive distortions getting on board or the assumption of a binary universe where it is all black OR white, light OR dark, right OR wrong, perhaps it's all spectrum. Each is simply one of two ends of the same observable spectrum. I say 'observable' because it's important to also remember that there is so much beyond our sensory ranges.

For example I can hear dog whistles (the little whistles to call dogs, not a dog whistling) which are supposed to be out of human hearing range, and I feel like I have a superpower.

Something shifty going on...

With just such diversity of perspectives informing each other, an exciting paradigm shift is occurring. Spirituality and science are arguably beginning to converge, in many ways.

Science (formerly known as Natural Philosophy until a Victorian re-brand) is a methodical pursuit of knowledge and understanding of our universe and everything in it. Scientific enquiry is a revolution in wondering, thinking, hypothesising, testing and drawing conclusion. It has led us to the most amazing inventions, discoveries and activities that have propelled our species from the dark ages to a kind of 'practical enlightenment'. Almost everything we take for granted today we owe at least in some parts to scientific minds - our tech, our vehicles, our domestic energy sources, our medicines, our food production and so on.

There are of course limitations to the method of scientific enquiry. There must be because science relies on replication and falsifiable hypotheses. This involves *measurement* and to measure something is to compare it or its chosen parts, relative to other things. This involves assumptions, decision making and judgement about *where, when, what* and *how* to measure. This is therefore a paradigmatic view of understanding - a perspective - and all paradigms and perspective exist because of their evolution and relativity to other perspectives and paradigms. They are fundamentally limited.

Thinking about measuring things is tricky. We cannot truly understand something by pre-judging its dimensions and deciding which bits to examine and which not to (if we even notice those). We thus pre-determine its nature by assuming boundaries - essentially what it is and what it is not.

So if we were to do this - measure and name a new thing according to its perceived boundaries and dimensions - we have not *understood* something that was pre-existing. We have *created* something out of it - and all too easily do we (mis)take this creative selection for the whole.

We would also have to create something to measure it with in the first place! In using a pre-existing tool - one that has determined the thingness of something else - we automatically bring in comparison, contrast, and judgement. What we end up with is not new understanding but a new sense of relativity of something to other things made of assumptions.

"Never ASSUME, because when you assume,
you make an ASS of U and ME."
Attributed to various people

Often we stick hard and fast to paradigms and schemas because they offer a sense of security and predictability in our world. When these are challenged we dismiss or trivialise the potential importance or significance in case our delicate worlds of lenses and mirrors are shattered.

If you have ever seen a ghost or some other paranormal occurrence, how quickly did you dismiss and 'explain away' the experience? I've seen countless instances of this happen. Yep not only have I seen 'ghosts' (for lack of a better term) and other curious things but I've witnessed others having their minds blown by strange encounters only to blink, shake their head and carry on as though nothing had occurred.

Other times, I have sat with a shivering, quivering former sceptic as they excitedly talked me through what anomaly had just happened, over and over and over, as though trying to get it straight in their doubting heads.

The point here is that a personal experience is just that - personal - and is very hard to refute if you were not the experiencer. Take your own experiences and those of others at face value, because otherwise there is a risk of inserting your own biases and obscuring *their* truth of what they experienced, and what it might mean for *them*.

Tolerance for intolerance...

Do you remember how Anxiety is an 'intolerance' to uncertainty? Well, intolerance is a much more insidious problem. It is important to realise and accept that we can be intolerant to other people's *views*. We must recognise that to be truly tolerant, we must be tolerant of intolerance itself.

For example, often we find that one person's milk makes another sick, e.g. for those who can't digest lactose, but does this mean that both parties should change their diet?

It's ok to dislike and not get along. Own it and accept it. It's not how you feel about a person that directs a relationship - it's how honest you are about those feelings and whether or not you act in accordance. For example, isn't it interesting that those whom we dislike so much, we so love to discuss? In fact, the two are quite positively-negatively correlated! Pun intended!

Furthermore, isn't it interesting how those who sit on the fence are often those who created the fence? Often, to take someone's story at 'face value', we would first have to consider which of their faces we were currently presented with.

As contrary as it may seem to be to you, some people like to be unhappy or ill - it is familiar and therefore predictable. It 'gives them a sense of meaning and also means they are given' (by caring others around them).

Consider that from their perspective, this helps them to meet certain needs - perhaps to feel 'safe', to gain intimacy or closeness with others and, also to hold 'significance' in some way.

When considering our own and other people's behaviour, choices and attitudes it's really helpful to draw on Freud's idea of the 'iceberg' - where we only see the tip of anyone's reality.

Ironically enough, many progressive psychologists today regard Freud's insight here as only the tip of an iceberg itself - where enormous scope for wider, deeper and shared unconscious influences was present but not explored.

You might say that the iceberg itself is in an ocean of influencing factors. Amusingly, Joseph Campbell (of aforementioned Hero's Journey fame) is said to have noted that *"Freud was fishing whilst sitting on a whale"*.

Anyhoo, back to the iceberg. I've drawn up a simplified and useful suggestion for contemplation (see opposite page). Imagine what is on your surface that others see... and consider what is underlying and influencing your visible self.

Consider the visible and invisible aspects of others too. This is a great way to help resolve conflict, achieve understanding and remove bias from situations.

I bet you another 10p that you can add so much more to this - and even get very specific to examine specific situations.

What would yours look like to your boss? Your mum? Your cat?

Check the little crab dude chillin' on top. Cute! He doesn't mind that the others back in Crabtown are all crabby and a bit nippy at times as he understands their aggression is a manifestation of unresolved existential angst.

(I know... Crabs don't live on icebergs... he's on sabbatical).

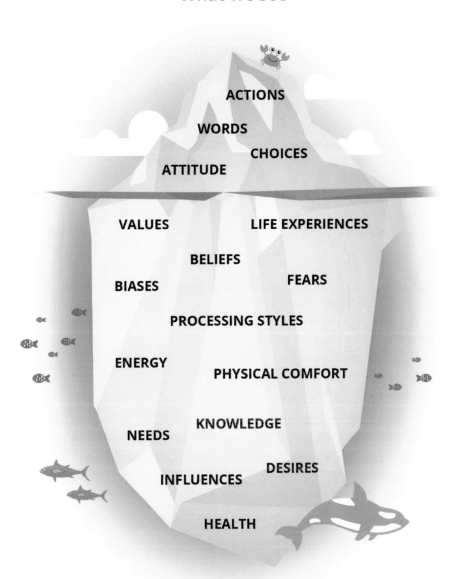

What we see

ACTIONS

WORDS

CHOICES

ATTITUDE

VALUES   LIFE EXPERIENCES

BELIEFS

BIASES   FEARS

PROCESSING STYLES

ENERGY

PHYSICAL COMFORT

KNOWLEDGE

NEEDS

DESIRES

INFLUENCES

HEALTH

What lies hidden below the surface

Power is Vulnerability and Vulnerability is Power

Challenging our thinking and our assumptions can leave us feeling a bit discombobulated. Being examined by others and also self-examination can leave us feeling exposed. It's important to notice any feelings that come up and consider what they are telling you - because they are reactions to the material in hand. Quite often, feelings of fear or suspicion lead us to shut down certain ways of thinking, especially if they are unfamiliar or challenge our perceptual comfort zones.

So where are we on this voyage to personal enlightenment? If adopting new thinking styles and taking risks is leaving you feeling a little vulnerable, that's ok. In fact, it's better than ok. It's GREAT!

Remember that you are the hero in your journey and that all heroes must face uncertainty, be challenged and be changed.

Enlightened teachers suffer - in fact they even choose suffering or seek it out. The suffering acts as a vehicle toward enlightenment where none of the horrors can maintain any grip on you. True freedom. Nothing can touch or harm you because you transcend *through* your vulnerability.

Vulnerability is not a weakness. In allowing yourself to be willingly vulnerable, you abandon fear. I think of vulnerability as being like a kind of emotional 'space' - it's an area of unknown and untested potential. Vulnerability is normal and we all have our vulnerabilities, however, what is unhelpful is in fearing that we will be exploited, that we will fall into the space and never return. It's the fear of something happening beyond our control that is the issue. We actually need vulnerability because it provides *space* for us to grow.

Similarly, when we come face to face with something we are really very afraid of and realise that we are OK despite the crushing panic, we actually gain resilience and grow into that space. On a certain level, this is how therapists help clients overcome phobias.

So, vulnerability is not the weakness it seems. Now let's talk about power. Power is not quite what it seems either. It is true that some people desire power above all else in life, in fact they may even desire power *over* all else in life and make a point of having it. Such people may well be in positions of high authority and income - such as politicians and world leaders, CEOs of huge companies and banks and so on. They may be inclined to abuse it too. History is full of examples of warlords and dictators, corruption and appropriation who all seized, wielded and abused power. This is a form of power that often comes not through consent but through deliberate design. To me, this is why so many 'leaders' really aren't leading at all, they are simply forcing their way to the front of the queue and taking everything for themselves. To me, this is not true power. This is malevolence.

There is a different kind of power dynamic that we might like to think about here. The ones we experience every day at home, work and play - including online. This kind of power dynamic actually does come from an unwritten contract of consent. For example, teachers are empowered to teach because children willingly (mostly) attend school. Power can only be had by someone if there is at least one other who is willing to grant it. This is a matter of choice and consent. It is a trade - and when you are trading, you are negotiating your terms. You always have the power to negotiate your terms (needs) with others - the trick is to know what they are.

THE THAFE WORD ITH
"EXTHITENTHIALIFM"

What in the name of flapdoodle is the relevance of this cartoon? Well...

When I was a model, I was often invited to represent fetish fashion, corsetry and all sorts of cutting-edge clothing. I travelled all over the world to clubs and shows where I met such an array of extraordinary people with unusual lives. I learned a lot about the BDSM world (best you look that NSFW acronym up in a private place), as a polite guest or by-stander. It just wasn't my 'thing', in case you are wondering but I appreciated that there was immense beauty in it. I would speak with dominatrices from across the globe with exceptional curiosity and respect - often for their business acumen, their understanding of 'play' as having therapeutic effects... and their utterly amazeballs footwear.

This is what I learned: True dominance comes from complete submission. The 'dom' was only ever in charge because the 'sub' permitted it. The sub could take away their consent at any time. A person who is a *willing* submissive to another, is the one holding all the true power, as only through their submissive role does the other person's power exist. Please note the key word of 'consent'. Bullies and abusers do not operate on consent!

Kinks aside, we all engage in power play in our relationships and that's ok. It's normal. Recognising when a power dynamic is not working for you is so important, and yet so few unhappy relationships ever work out a new one. It may not be 'dominance and/or submission' but a rather more subtle balancing act of everyone's expectations and considerations.

Arguments that break out over tasks such as who forgot to take the bin out, or who fed the cat a donut and so on, are usually little things that explode in an outpouring of anger, despair and Anxiety that's out of all proportion, right? This is often because those little things are actually really about the BIG things. Recognising emotional reactions to all the little things can tell you an enormous amount about whether or not your needs are being met and if the dynamic needs re-negotiating.

If your relationship with Anxiety is not working, then perhaps it's time to consider why. Are you fighting with it? Hiding from it? What is the power dynamic? Remember too that Anxiety is the experience you *have*, it's not a force you can actually fight with or hide from because you are creating it. The only real option is to accept it for what it is and work from there. It can't dominate you because if you don't submit to it - if you accept it alongside you, you can even move forward and take the lead.

Surrendering to that which you struggle against (in this case Anxiety) means that you stop fulfilling its power over you. Surrendering is not the same as succumbing to. It is in fact the opposite - it is the acceptance of the situation and resulting ability to co-exist (unharmed and uninfluenced).

Mind-blowing peace

As any old guru will tell you, the highest experience of the conscious being is generally understood to be a direct experience of 'non-duality' or 'Oneness of everything', deep interconnectedness with all things - where there is no separation between you and everything else.

Mind-blowing peace, in an ironic sort of way.

The direct experience of oneness is like being struck still to your core by the sheer awesomeness of infinite space - and surrendering completely into it. Enlightenment comes not after the accumulation of lots of knowledge but after much contemplation of our thoughts and the eventual abandoning of all thought - surrendering to the mystery.

It wouldn't be Ironic Fundamentalism without delving in to 'practical metaphysics' and gaining that meta perspective on what it all means, and how to enhance your experience of transmuting your Anxiety into a pathway to your own Enlightenment.

Space-time Continuum Conundrum

Curiously, space is defined in terms of time and, time is defined in terms of space. This conundrum is all about our human desire to measure the crap out of everything. The time taken to travel between two points of location and the distance covered between two points in time is 'relative'.

Therefore, time and space are dimensional in a united continuum. Now, perhaps here we can solve one of life's great mysteries - why does a builder's schedule always overrun?

Have you ever looked up at the stars and been overwhelmed with awe? At the stars themselves but more so at the vastness in which they have been made to manifest? This vast nothingness isn't nothing... it is the pure potential from where all 'things that are' come from and are held in existence - it is everything that isn't (but could be).

Let's think of how we too are mostly 'empty space' - or, 'potential'. Our bodies too are mostly space rather than stuff. Sure, the physical stuff we are made of is indeed particles, atoms, chemicals and so on - in fact it's the same stuff that the stars are comprised of. We are made of star stuff. But the spaces between each particle is enormously vast in comparison to the amount of space taken up by the physical stuff, to help put this in perspective, the human body is actually more like 99.9999999% space and it is estimated that if we lost our 'space' and condensed ourselves in to the physical stuff, we would be at most, the size of a dust particle. Cool space dust. But dust. So... why do we tend to overlook the 99.9999999% of what we actually are? Why do we assume it is somehow 'empty' and without relevance? Perhaps instead, we might consider that this is our potential? That by placing our conscious awareness (our 'Go') here instead, we might create or manifest anything?

There is of course, lots of debate surrounding the nature of stuff and space and consciousness but this often-cited quote attributed to Erwin Schödinger (of entangled cat fame) really inspires wonder: *"Consciousness cannot be accounted for in physical terms. For consciousness is absolutely fundamental. It cannot be accounted for in terms of anything else."* What might it mean for us, if we are to shift our thinking from the materialist view of stuff to one of consciousness as central and underpinning our reality?

It seems that whether or not we use this or that scientific lens, at the heart of the universe lies absurdity; as though this whole expansive experience we call life is in fact one big hilarious wind-up. If we consider the implications of infinite possibility, our existence right now as we share these words (and potential to keep existing later today) is absolutely staggeringly awesome.

Think about the following: By virtue of infinity there are finite things, including infinite finite things (can you imagine what that would look like?).

If something is binary it means it belongs to the assumption of 1 *or* 0. So, if 1, it means there is always the potential of 0 and vice versa. For example, in a coin toss a 'Heads up result' is only ever up *if* Tails is down, and vice versa (and of course down *is* down 'because' of up).

If there is infinite potential, then all things *are* and *aren't* at the same time. Of course, this is where the role of the 'observer' comes in. When the awareness of a conscious mind is focused on any potential, that 1 and 0 becomes 1 *or* 0. Here, the potential manifests as an observable creation. Is dark the absence of light? Is light the absence of dark? Are dark and light the same experience only differentiated by who is looking?

If this is all sounding a bit philosophical, a bit mystical, a bit well 'meta', then you are right it totally is. It is also science. As quantum physicists and mathematicians will testify, the further down the rabbit hole we go, the weirder the science gets with contradictions at every turn and sometimes results in a necessity to suspend logic and rationality.

As I'm not going to pretend to be a physicist I'll keep it brief and to this point: Various experiments show that there is a paradox in the nature of reality, that for example in work made most famous by quantum physicist Richard Feynman, photons of light can exist in two states at the same time (as both a wave function and a particle before collapsing in to one or t'other). Furthermore, that said photon of light might not even settle in to being one or the other, 'this or that' *until there is an observer to make the distinction.*

Similarly, in the good old Schrödinger Cat thought experiment (there was no real half/half zombie kitty... just a thought experiment), where a hypothetical cat in a mystery box was either poisoned or not (!). Perhaps intended as an example of *'reductio ad absurdum'* (which is philosopher speak for a proposition that reduces to the absurd) where both possible cats co-existed until the box was opened and an observation made, and one cat would manifest over the other. But there we have it at least as one science fact... that cats are champs at sitting in boxes and being contrary buttholes.

Chaos is the foundation of order

True chaos creates all order - because all possibilities are potential in a true state of chaos. There cannot be any order unless it exists within a state of non-ordered contrast. There must be something from which order can be constructed. Without random occurrence, no order could ever be established from chance, and even then 'order' is constructed by our perception of patterns. True chaos must create perceived order, otherwise, it is behaving according to a rule that avoids such.

> *"One must still have creative chaos in oneself*
> *to be able to give birth to a dancing star."*
> **Friedrich Nietzsche**

We are everything and nothing. We are one.

Nothingness is not bad.

It is simply the contrasting term we have for *is-ness* or 'form'. It holds ready potential - perhaps we could think of it as is the precursor state to creation e.g. before there was a baby, there was no baby. Also, a baby is not made up of babies, it is made of billions of other things that are in a constant state of flux and change; conceptually 'baby' is just a label in the English language.

We often think of is-ness and isn't-ness as being concrete, foundational factual states but even mathematics is bendy and doesn't offer the kind of base line level of 'fact' that we might expect. The proof of $1 + 1 = 2$ is actually a lengthy work of philosophy. Like logic, maths is actually based on axioms or assumptions that are unprovable.

Similarly, science as a whole is based on assumptions and hypotheses for likely answers, not absolute answers. There is no ultimate truth as demonstrated through any discipline.

They are used to help us predict how our world and the stuff in it works - but they do not actually define or 'explain' anything absolutely. These studies are like cartography - they are charts that allows us to outline, predict and conjecture. Like how a treasure map is not the treasure nor even is it the destination itself.

Ontology is like curating objects in a museum - grouped by what traits? Same colour? Age? Where found? Used in food preparation? Made from animal parts? Contains a gemstone?

What does this mean? Is Life, The Universe and Everything a trick of the light? An illusion? Is there a conscious mind observing the whole thing unfold?

Is it someone else's mind or is it your mind? My mind? OUR mind?

Consciousness and the Explanatory Gap

Here's another conundrum. The explanatory gap (coined by philosopher Joseph Levine) is the mystery of how the physical brain/body/world gives rise to the felt experience of consciousness? This is also known as the 'hard problem' of consciousness coined by another philosopher David Chalmers.

The implications of this area of thinking and research is of interest to many disciplines including psychology, religion, physics, neurobiology and Artificial Intelligence. In this 'gap' we find that so many theories fall. As thinkers and worriers, we also might fall into this gap feeling lost forever without an explanation of how 'this becomes that'. Keeping the fundamental irony and interconnectedness of all things in mind I propose once again... that the 'gap' is not empty. That much like all else in the Universe, consciousness is a spectrum of experience.

Ancient philosophers (and many, many since) have proposed that consciousness (in its general sense) is ubiquitous to reality. That 'all things are mental' - everything in the universe is made up of or contains 'mind'. This is a theory generally known as 'panpsychism' which literally means 'all psyche' (or 'all mind').

In the 20th century luminary astrophysicist Professor Arthur Eddington experimentally confirmed Einstein's theory of relativity and challenged the status quo by aligning himself with a theory of panspsychism. He purported that there was a gap of understanding between what matter *does* and actually *is*. Stating in 1928 that *"The stuff of the world is mind-stuff"* and that consciousness could not arise from non-consciousness, he suggested that this 'gap' was the realm of consciousness.

This wonderful idea of 'panpsychism' is of course a debate, however, the general theory prevails today with many leading thinkers who are researchers in cutting edge science and spirituality.

Where quantum physics is telling us about observer effects on stuff 'out there' in photons and in boxes, we can apply this effect too - 'in here' - in our consciousness. The meaning from this is that we must be *observing* our conscious experiences as we are having (or perhaps doing) them - in order to make them a reality. That the key to 'manifesting your best life' is the same as the key to all Creation - you must simply be self-aware. Present in the moment to be aware of Unity.

Hermetically (un)Sealed

I first came in to contact with the Hermetic Principles in my teens. For whatever reason, at 14 I felt I was having a 'mid-life' crisis. I had no time for pop music or just 'hanging out'. I was already reading books on hypnosis, the mind, ancient religion and paranormal experience. It turned out my crisis was existential angst about Life, The Universe and Everything. I was a 14 year old girl, and so I did not buy a sports car.

I wanted to 'know' that there was more meaning to my existence than being obliged to purchase the latest albums or follow the fictitious hum-drum misery of soap characters. At this point I was kind of 'scooped up' by enthusiastic Christians and began attending their church but I didn't last long there.

After a year or so, I was made to feel rather unwelcome after asking questions about the fundamental nature of God, why there was so much misogyny in the Old Testament and why for a religion that didn't talk about sex, why was everyone particularly bothered about gay people's private activities? I just didn't get the spiritual significance of being a jerk to others over their gender or sexuality. Also, I wanted answers about the BIG stuff and no-one was willing to entertain me. I think I was regarded as a nuisance and so I was told (at that age of 15) that my 'ideas were dangerous to other young people'. It was suggested that my inclination toward metaphorical interpretation of scripture was 'no better than a Gnostic'.

Anyhoo, after hearing about this mysterious heretical 'Gnostic' way of thinking and being a philosophical rebel (I was 'so cool', yes), I latched onto that word 'Gnostic' and ran for the hermetic hills and caves of secret wisdom. I found myself in Waterstones bookshop in Glasgow. It was close enough and they had a great Mind, Body, Spirit section, plus I only had a bus pass. My longtime friend Morgana (quoted in this book) and I spent hours and hours and hours here, to the point of starting to feel like we were merging with the furniture. Maybe we did.

I became a tiny bit extremely obsessed with alternative 'apocryphal' scripture especially the Gnostic Gospels and... *Hermeticism.*

> *"Birth is not the beginning of life - only of an individual awareness. Change into another state is not death - only the ending of this awareness."*
> **Hermes Trismegistus**

So... what the flup is Hermeticism?

Hermeticism is an ancient philosophy that explains 'how the Universe works' - in a beautifully poetic, yet straight up simple way. Attributed to *Hermes Trismegistus* the material is considered to be over 2,000 years old and a precursor to Gnostic Christianity and other mystic traditions. Hermeticism is increasingly popular today as a rediscovered guide to personal development and spiritual growth.

Hermes Trismegistus is not only revered as great - but 3 x great. *(Hermes the 'thrice-great magician')* and is kind of a metaphysical character because he may or may not have existed physically (there is debate) but either way, serves as an embodiment of the wisdom that has been handed down over the millennia despite the risk of heretical crime and punishment. Some followers of Hermeticism believe he was a real person who was deified as Thoth (the Egyptian God of Wisdom and Writing), others say that he was an ancient master teacher whose letters and writings have been emerging under other names since the Italian Renaissance and influenced great minds including Leonardo da Vinci. Hermes, of course is also the God of Wisdom and the messenger of the gods in ancient Greece and so whatever the popular mythology or ancient history, there is an incredibly rich interconnected depth to received Hermetic wisdom.

As I was coming close to finishing writing this book, I had a distinct and vivid dream that the IF approach to Anxiety was in harmony with Hermetic philosophy.

Given that Hermes Trismegistus probably didn't exist as a singular person and that there are no exact undisputed originals, and that there are countless books and materials exploring Hermetic writings, it's hard to attribute precise quotes.

Helpfully, when researching online, I discovered that not only is Hermeticism truly thriving in the modern esoteric world, but that many enthusiasts were referencing something called *The Kybalion*.

The Kybalion was published in 1908 by unnamed authors under the wonderfully mysterious credit 'Three Initiates'. This book (still in print and available online) was essentially a (then) contemporary distillation of Hermetic philosophy and it suggested 7 principles or 'laws of the universe'. I have attempted to share the aphorisms and ideas here for you to gain even more perspective and see how all these 'modern' ideas are a reincarnation of old.

It is so empowering to see how our journey and all the aforementioned science, psychology and spiritually can come together.

The Hermetic Principles

1 - Mentalism

"THE ALL is MIND; The Universe is Mental."
The Kybalion

The universe is a living conscious mind and everything in it is connected through it. An infinite field of cosmic consciousness in which all things are manifest. All energy, power and matter are mastered by *mind*.

(This first principle is considered to be the 'master key' to understanding.)

Remember the first words of this book? "An anxious mind is a living mind".

Furthermore, that as an anxious person you have the gifts of extreeeme mental rehearsal, imagination and hypothesising? If all things are mind, then you are deeply infinitely connected to all things and the phrase 'no-thing to worry about' becomes ever more meaningful.

2 - Correspondence

"As above, so below; as below, so above."
The Kybalion

There is always a corresponding 'other' to all things, a shared entangled existence, including the known and the unknown. Just as the electron microscope shows us the tiny worlds of particles so too does the Hubble telescope show us the vast worlds of the cosmos. Think of the corresponding reflected sameness of microcosm and macrocosm, and of your inner world and the outer observable world. Each *corresponds* to the other.

Remember the lenses? From Petri dish to Opera house? From personal relationships to global politics? For every little worry or wonder you experience, there is the unfathomably bigger corresponding one which is simultaneously taking care of itself. Remind yourself... 'It's ok, the Universe has got this on all levels'.

3 - Vibration

"Nothing rests; everything moves; everything vibrates."
The Kybalion

Different manifestations of mind, matter and spirit all vibrate - from tiny electrons to planets. Everything in us is in motion and all things have a specific vibration.

We see this in the strange beauty of cymatics (the study of visible sound and vibrations), in the resonance of rocks and crystals, in musical tones, in the wavelength of colour and so on. It is considered that spirit (or conscious self-awareness) has the very highest vibration and so, the 'higher' we raise (vibrate) our consciousness, the more enlightened we become.

Remember the 'explanatory gap' and how gaps are not empty? Just as when a perfectly tuned string on a musical instrument is played, others that are also perfectly tuned to the same note will also vibrate in unison with the one being played.

Think too about how you are never alone with your Anxiety - that every similar soul shares the experience of the other, through resonance. You are 'felt' and shared across the universe.

4 - Polarity

"Everything is Dual; everything has poles; everything has its pair of opposites; like and unlike are the same; opposites are identical in nature, but different in degree; extremes meet; all truths are but half-truths; all paradoxes may be reconciled."
The Kybalion

Everything is and isn't at the same time where opposites are spectrums of the same thing with many degrees between them, e.g. light and dark, hot and cold, love and hate, large and small, positive and negative, doubt and faith, fear and growth.

Think back to our many spectrums of experience we have looked at and the inherent choice of interpretation we actually have. Also consider the times when you are holding those opposing, conflicting thoughts or feelings at the same time and the 'gap' between them.

Think too about your ability to imagine the worst, must also mean you could imagine the best. That crushing Anxiety is also your secret power. Reconciling the paradox of Anxiety as a force for creative purpose is pretty cool, right?

5 - Rhythm

> *"Everything flows, out and in; everything has its tides;*
> *all things rise and fall; the pendulum-swing manifests*
> *in everything; the measure of the swing to the right is the*
> *measure of the swing to the left; rhythm compensates."*
> **The Kybalion**

Everything has a 'to' and 'fro', ebb and flow, a swing forward and backward. Applying this to all mind, matter and energy again reveals such wealth of potential and how we can direct our intentions and expectations as there is always an action and reaction.

Thinking on the pendulum further, it swings left and then right and then left again... or right and then left and then right again. It is in the rhythm that direction is established.

Remember the changing nature of our physical sensations, our thoughts and emotions as they ebb and flow in relation to one another? Where we experience crisis, we also see opportunity reveal itself. It's all about perception and what we choose to focus our attention on.

6 - Cause and Effect

"Every Cause has its Effect; every Effect has its Cause;
everything happens according to Law; Chance is but
a name for Law not recognised; there are many
planes of causation, but nothing escapes the Law."
The Kybalion

Every cause has an effect, every effect has its cause and therefore nothing happens by 'chance'. Remember the importance of positive risk-taking? Think of yourself as a cause rather than an effect.

When you want a cake you make the effort by doing the needed actions - collecting and mixing the ingredients. You then put it in the oven and wait. You don't get in the oven with it, and you don't keep stirring and adding until it somehow just becomes a cake. You sit back and *allow it to rise.*

When you want to see a flower bloom you put in the gardening effort and then sit back and *allow it to grow.* You literally wait for it to *unfold* its petals.

7 - Gender

"Gender is in everything: everything has its Masculine
and Feminine Principles; Gender manifests on all planes."
The Kybalion

Everything has masculine and feminine principles. Gender manifests on all planes. All things are both masculine and feminine. Creation is possible through the principle of gender where each person has both male and female gender and has the power for creation and recreation within themselves. This is where our creativity springs from.

Remember too that what other people think of you is a construct. Gender is a construct that gives a false sense of being 'this' OR 'that'. We are all both. We are One.

Again, think of how Anxiety affects our decisions based on masculine OR feminine ways of being, thinking and doing. Instead of subscribing to one, adopt the attitude of both and find a balanced approach.

Through the Keyhole!

Keys are such interesting symbols. They come in all sorts of forms - from familiar metal tools to open metal locks, huge iron ones and tiny delicate ones on a diary or child's jewellery box. They can be plastic rectangles such as bank 'key cards' or access cards for buildings; they can be codes, scales that direct music, they can be questions or clues to solving a mystery and they can also be people. We often think of 'key janglers' as people who habitually carry and fiddle with a set of keys making them tinkle, clash and jangle as a reminder of their authority in being the key-keeper. Keyhole silhouettes are a long-held trope of voyeurism, of hidden watchers.

Keys hold a sense of power to access that which is guarded or protected. They remind us of things that are hidden, secret or precious and they are symbols of both that which is 'kept' and that which is set free. Keys are our totemic permission for potential.

I love old antique keys. They are one of the many curiosities I collect. To me, when a key no longer has a designated lock it therefore has the potential to open anything, anywhere. When I was mid-way through writing this book, I had a dream that explained this idea to me and I should urge everyone to find and carry just such a mystery key. On waking, I realised the connection between Ironic Fundamentalism and the Hermetic Principles... and here we are.

The Hermetic Principles are keys that give you ultimate CHOICE.

By observing the fundamental irony in all things, we can truly utilise these 7 keys to frame and understand any aspect of our Anxiety. Here we can choose, observe, compensate, engineer and even design the experience and outcomes we want. It is personal alchemy - 'mental transmutation'.

> *"Mind (as well as metals and elements) may be transmuted,*
> *from state to state; degree to degree; condition to condition;*
> *pole to pole; vibration to vibration.*
> *True Hermetic Transmutation is a Mental Art."*
> **The Kybalion**

This applies way beyond Anxiety of course - it applies to all things. It's just so relevant here right now in this book because you are likely sitting on a goldmine of untapped alchemical skills. We all remain *subject to the laws,* but we can choose to not become *objects of effect.*

Hermetic masters use these principles and train all their lives to have the ritualistic habits and expansive emotional and mental talents that Anxiety has gifted to you.

This is what IF proposes we do with our Anxiety as a dojo-like training ground. As an anxious person you already hold the key skills for manifesting your Enlightenment. Ironic, right? You just need to adjust your orientation.

Alchemy? Universe? All a bit magical woo-woo? Need a bit of familiar text-book science? That's cool... it's all cool. It's all the same.

What IF... you don't have to choose between science and spirituality?

There has long been assumed to be a gap between spiritual and scientific thinking - and belief. It's as though to follow one means you must exclusively deny the other, like a shitty relationship where you are made to choose between your other half and your best friend. Now why would anyone think this was healthy, loving or even reasonable? Unsurprisingly, such relationships are at the root of so much pain and Anxiety. Quit now, give up the addiction to exclusive ideological subscription - it does not work.

The Gap is closing. The theoretical, ideological and social gap between science and spirituality is closing. It is closing because of the BIG questions. Namely, the age-old conundrum of consciousness, and out of this paradigmatic shift, comes a new blend of thinking.

"Religion to me is science, and science is religion."
Ada Lovelace

The hidden or mystical side of religion and spirituality is no longer for the few 'initiated' or privileged devotees. It is open to all. The modern approach for social inclusion (over privilege, gender, age, class and race) also make the inner mysteries accessible like never before. For example, no longer will a person's perceived gender exclude them.

There is always a simultaneous trend both for and against the status quo. If you want to be a rebel in 2020, go to church. The trend for Atheism is no longer the rebellion it was ten years ago with people tending to choose personal development over aggressive debate. With the rise in interest of philosophy and how to think, rather than what to think, those people drawn to such big questions are rewriting the gospels to be more inclusive.

Many hitherto 'traditional' scientists are also starting to converge toward the mystical - from neuroscience to cosmology (as above, so below*) and quantum mechanics, it's all getting rather metaphysical with the quest for understanding human consciousness growing steadily in the laboratories of medicine, technology, psychology and disciplines that deal with quantum physics. The materialist paradigm is shifting to explore the 'hard problem of consciousness' and nonduality. Science is becoming ever more spiritually relevant and exciting with amazing new disciplines like 'neurotheology' at the forefront of modern thinking.

The Hermetic principle of correspondence "as above so below" relates to the microcosm and macrocosm of reality, just as both science and philosophy examine the same questions from neutron to nebula. The inner and outer mysteries, from ancient mystical schools to contemporary life coaching and from hieroglyphs to emojis, it's all the same age-old wisdom re-emerging under the shifting paradigms of cultural lenses. So too are the little questions and the Big Questions your Anxiety is teaching you about.

Spirituality is good for your mental health. Research is showing that during religious or spiritual activities like prayer and meditation certain areas of the brain are turned on and others shut down with changes in the balance of neurotransmitters. For example, during prayer, neurochemicals including serotonin, dopamine and GABA all increase, while stress hormones such as cortisol and norepinephrine (adrenaline) decrease. The temporal lobes and limbic structures are shown to be involved in religious experience with the basal ganglia involved in states of euphoria. In those persons who have a strong sense of religious faith, their brains look different to scientists from those who do not have such faith. This is throwing out many questions on the direction of cause and effect, e.g. is a person religious because their brain was predisposed to it? or has the brain developed because of their faith?

The explanatory gap, the social gaps and the methodology-of-enquiry gaps are closing, unity is ever more in reach to those who seek it. We no longer must pick a proverbial side. We no longer need to dwell in the angst of Anxiety on what to think. We are free. As the brilliant Eddington also said:

"You will understand the true spirit neither of science nor of religion unless seeking is placed in the forefront."
Arthur Eddington, Science and the Unseen World

CHAPTER THREE

SOME RATHER IFFY ADVICE FOR COMMON PROBLEMS

So many of our anxieties are rooted in a fear of rejection by others, through worry over our place in the world, our being different or maybe even not different enough, finding our purpose and our worth... and so on.

So, let's consider:

Average is a mean illusion!

Every body and every mind is beautiful. Fact.

Beauty norms are an illusion. Mental or physical. Every cell that makes up every single body is a unique expression of the universe, creating itself. Regardless of height, weight and other measurable things, immeasurable beauty lives in the whole-ness and joy of every living being. Love your body and know that it is astonishingly exquisite - as this is exactly how it has been made.

What does an average mind or body look like? Where would we find one?

All our notions of 'normal' and ideal are illusions - in many cases these are illusions on which we all collaborate! Averages are concepts that only exist because of human VARIETY - how ironic!

One of my favourite ideas is attributed to Albert Einstein and says, *"The true sign of intelligence is not knowledge but imagination."*

Statistics are a great tool for understanding populations or groups - but they do not define any one person in any way! This is where we often get ourselves all wound up. Thinking we should tend toward any 'average' or 'mean' leads us in fear and to think unkindly about ourselves (and sometimes others too). The 'mean' or 'average' of any set is more like a numerically derived guesstimate of what's there - and actually is less likely to apply to anyone involved!

When we 'deviate' or differ in some way from the average, we are simply demonstrating that we are all individuals that cannot be accurately charted. So, celebrate being a deviant! It's natural and ideal!

How others see you is none of your business

Worrying about how others see you? What they think about you? There isn't anything wrong with that feeling, it's perfectly normal to wonder what other people might think of us. But you should not actually spend a lot of time on these thoughts - it really isn't any of your business. Honestly, this is not a telling off statement, but instead is one that should free you from feeling any kind of responsibility to finding out.

Understand, first, the reason why other people's thoughts or opinions of you are none of your concern. It's important to remember that just as you have your own personal outlook and experience, so does each other person you meet. Next time you are tempted to eavesdrop, just don't. You will not learn anything except that you are overly concerned about judging others for *possibly* judging you, in a situation where you don't have all the pieces of the jigsaw and its guesswork at best. Many famous literary stories including Shakespeare's Othello warn us of eavesdropping because half-heard, half-understood comments can lead to fully realised tragedy.

Furthermore, what they think of you is not you anyway - it's that individual's impression of you. Their impression is comprised of their own unique biases - formed from their own circumstance, their direct experience with you, and their previous experience with other comparative people. And those people are also just a bunch of biases pulled together to paint an impressionist's portrait. It's all rather 2 dimensional!

"O wad some Power the giftie gie us, to see oursels as ithers see us!"
Robert Burns, To A Louse

My favourite line from my homeland's national bard. It is part of Scottish schooling to learn and recite Burns from a very young age, where we would win certificates (and the teary-eyed pride of tartan grandparents). In particular, this line struck me like no other, nor any ever since.

For as long as I can remember, it has inspired me to think about the concept of 'self' and all those other 'selves' that engage in a collaborative perceptual illusion of perceiving one another. The notion that there is any 'self' to perceive is a seriously iffy concept, as there is really very little consistency to go on beyond memories that link our experiences together across time. But this is a huge topic, so here I'm focusing in on the idea of how we think of ourselves, according to reflections around us - what we see and what we think others see.

Self as a reference

When we look in a mirror or other reflective surface, we see a reverse of that which is arguably 'real' and what others see when looking straight at us. Our left becomes our right and vice versa, so right away, we have this entire concept of self - through the filter of our looks - quite literally backwards.

Perhaps this is why so many of us find it uncomfortable looking at photos of ourselves - we are actually the 'wrong' way around. Of course, looking in the mirror is always subject to light and how shadows are cast, making dramatic differences in our bone structure and fullness of face - try it yourself, taking a torch and experimenting with different angles in the mirror. What do you see? Bearing in mind that you are completely the other way around for how others see you, is anything in your image ever really 'fixed'? Or, is it all in the context of light in the environment, angles, the eye of the beholder and also how you are *feeling* when you look? Not only will your emotions dictate how you interpret what you *fixate* on, but your face will hold that emotion in the form of tension, expression and facial micro-expressions.

Paranormal enthusiasts often engage within a psychomanteum ('mirror gazing') where they simply gaze at their reflection to watch their own features morph seemingly into the faces of departed others, looking back at us through the mirror from some other dimension.

Psychology speculates that the perception of our faces morphing is perhaps less to do with ghosts or spirits and instead is due to the Troxler Effect (where our attention starts to fade or blur information surrounding our point of focus) coupled with our evolved sense of facial detection - an innate, unconscious threat-finding ability - where possible faces and especially unfamiliar ones can be seen hiding in any surface. Better to mistakenly see the face of a lion hiding in a bush and run, than to simply see a quirky arrangement of leaves and get eaten. Mirror Gazing is quite a remarkable phenomenon, and whether you believe in ghosts or not, the morphing will still likely work for you. I have engaged in it and also guided 'ghost hunters' in this with interesting results.

Give it a go and 'see' who you become, and try to determine the exact point at which you are no longer 'you'...that is the 'you' you recognise and assume is the 'correct' version. What this shows us again is the impermanent nature of being - that there is no fixed 'you', only the ones we create and fixate upon... and fixation masks reality as it stifles growth.

So, who we are is not a constant, and is as changing as the sky upon the surface of water. As Narcissus would testify, gazing too closely and too long can be fatal, yet perhaps the deeper wisdom is that self-reflection ultimately leads to the complete dissolution or 'death' of self. Rather than being a cautionary tale or vanity issue, the story of Narcissus is one of enlightenment - there is no "you".

That you might use all your time and energy trying to establish an identity and pointlessly fix that identity in time - and furthermore, where that still water acts as a mirror, it too is impermanent, unstable and to not recognise this is to risk drowning.

After all, we are all 'you' to someone else and there is a point in time and space where any part of you starts to become something else - for example, when we absorb medication or when stroking a cat - which are spaces between the atoms and which are the cat? What is giving rise to the shared experience?

Others as a reference

Our relationships also act as mirrors, and when our relationships change for whatever reason, we can feel hurt or compromised. We were seeing ourselves based on how those others treated us - not how they actually saw or regarded us. This way, self-image is built on assumptions about the behaviour of others and their motivations toward us.

Therefore, when people leave you, you hurt and feel you must have done something 'wrong' to bring about the change - perhaps you are no longer attractive/useful to them? When they seem not to care, it's really about them - not you. The chances are it is their reflection of themselves that has inspired the change, not 'you'.

This can be extremely challenging as our sense of self according to others is what often provides our self-confidence. Like two mirrors eternally reflecting each other, trying to establish any truth to reality is an impossible task.

So often as reflections of ourselves change we tend to focus on questioning who we are - and often overlook the changes occurring in the perspective holder. Change is reflected, and so we may in fact have an altered perspective of the actual changes as well.

If friends or lovers or relations should ever leave us, it is time for multi-source 'reflection'. We can reflect on who we are and build a more positive image than ever before by looking at and examining several points of reflection - from the past, present, and even our intended future. Consider your own:

- History of your own projects/career (what was the motivation/ result each time?)

- History of friendships (how they begun/ended each time. What values were exposed?)

- What/who is important to you now? (What/who do you think of first in the morning and last at night?)

- What do you aspire to? (Not simply ambition per se as this relies on unhelpful comparisons with others... instead consider aspiration... what do you want to be within yourself?) and what holds you back or pushes you forward?

This is the stuff of true personal development.

If you should ever find yourself or your work the subject of critique, remember that this simply means that you are doing something interesting - and worthy of discussion.

Focus on the positives but also take any 'negatives' as ironic positives too. 'Flip' them to reinforce your position as someone of influence (intended or not) and that anything useful in the comments can be used to aid self-reflection and future refinement. Anyone taking the time to comment is a compliment to your potency, whether it feels like it or not!

"When the critics disagree the artist is in accord with himself."
Oscar Wilde

It all leads us to think again that there is little point in worrying about what others think of us - and that anything other than self-acceptance and aspiration to grow, is a reflection of egoic concern (and therefore pulling in the opposite direction of growth).

Personal Attractiveness

There is a LOT of Anxiety surrounding our bodies. How attractive we feel we are to others provokes a great deal of Anxiety in most of us. I use the term 'personal attractiveness' rather than 'physical' or 'sexual' attractiveness because attraction is not one dimensional. It's not a 'this or that', 'is or isn't' situation.

Interpersonal attraction involves many practical factors such as familiarity (how often we see each other), similarity (having things in common) and geographical proximity (the literal distance or closeness to one another), although with online relationships and the advance of technology, this latter factor is perhaps less powerful than it was pre-social media days.

The desirability of personality traits is also not as straightforward as a 'yes or no' checklist of 'must haves'. Some of us are attracted to the classic 'GSOH' yet others have little time for jokes and want candour and sobriety. Some people are attracted to confidence and boldness, others are entirely put off by the same. The list of traits is endless and the interplay between what we each seek and offer likely arise from our changing needs and desires in life.

What personality traits are you attracted to in others? Has that ever changed? What do you get out of it? What need is being satisfied? Security? A sense of belonging? Social significance? Fun and stimulation? What else? A mix? What are they getting from you?

How we feel about our bodies emotionally and how we then embody those emotions leads us to carry ourselves with poise and confidence or otherwise. For example, a teenager who is feeling insecure about her changing body shape might begin to hide her shape with baggy clothes and rounded shoulders. Someone who has recently won a medal for their body building physique will likely present the detail of their physique as clearly as possible. In these examples, choices are being made about how to present the bodies - according to whether or not the person's emotions support being 'seen' and potentially 'judged' by others.

Consider how you carry and present yourself and ask yourself 'what belief about myself am I reinforcing?'. Is it an anxious need to hide or is it motivation to grow? Is it a fear of rejection or a desire for appreciation? How does this make you feel?

There is no right or wrong way to look or feel or behave. The point here is in developing self-awareness of the link between feelings and behaviour. It's about choice. Choose the behaviour that supports how you *want* to feel, not the behaviour that reinforces how you don't want to feel.

Many of us become totally preoccupied with how 'fat or thin', 'tall or short' we are. How our curves and lines measure up, even how vascular we are or aren't. It can often seem like there is an ideal 'out there' that determines what we 'should' look like and strive for - but this is an illusion of shared cultural lenses. This is where 'norms' are misleading because we are each our own normal in ourselves. Norms aren't somehow 'correct' or 'right' they are simply trending 'right now'. For example, the female figure throughout the history of Western art has been consistently directed by the 'male gaze' (the specific masculine heterosexual point of view of those who were mostly making the art). But the changing trends for 'skinniness' and 'curviness' that we tend to fixate on are not actually at odds with one another.

Whether ancient Grecian marble statues, the painting of Rubens' ample ladies (where we get the term 'Rubenesque'), the slender fairy-tale waifs of the pre-Raphaelites, the elongated figures of Erte in the 1920s, the curvy pin-ups of the 1950s... and the changing figures of fashion today, they all have much in common. They may look different in terms of their weight, but their proportional bust-waist-hip ratios are all more or less the same, it's the same *fat distribution* that is maintained by these artists, not what dress size they might be.

There is a beautiful irony that we are all more alike than we can see and more diverse than we can imagine. The truth is that we exist in a universe of ultimate diversity. Without genetic diversity we just wouldn't exist at all - if we were carbon copies of each other, our species would have died out long ago.

It is perfectly normal to be diverse just as much as it is to conform with the apparent norms of the day because norms are fluid and are ever-changing over time and social influence. Regardless of what we think we see in ourselves and each other, we all unconsciously share certain tendencies too. Just as there is a universal mathematical formula in the spirals of seashells, flower petals, and galaxies, it is also right here within us too, in the arrangement of our faces, bodies and DNA. It is from this baseline blueprint that both our sameness and our uniqueness occur. However it manifests, it is a celebration of both individual and collective growth.

There is also a very peculiar Anxiety around being 'sexy'. A sense of historical shame that has led us to live with a cultural mindset of horrendous body judgement. Despite sex as the foundation of our existence (including closeness to one another, not just procreation), a desire to be regarded as sexually attractive is often considered to be somehow 'desperate', 'deviant' or indicating psychological 'damage'. For so many, sexuality in itself has been denied, suppressed and vilified through the ages leading to persecution and execution. So much so that many of us still fear, avoid or shy away from physically identifying with sex at all.

Yet we elevate it in select others. It's really odd that celebrities such as pop stars and actors are perceived as being *positively* sexy - in a kind of permitted sense (we might call them 'professionally sexy'). Yet certain other famous people (e.g. politicians) and non-famous people identifying with sexuality are often considered to be unwell or socially unsuitable, even dangerous - and this has been especially true in Western culture for women and all those in the LGBQTA+ communities. From sex itself to the act of breastfeeding infants, it is particularly ironic that women's bodies are so ubiquitously denigrated considering that all our mums had at least enough sex that we can all be here and be ashamed about it.

It's a curious thing that we are so shy of something so fundamental, so literally creative.

We are each personally and collectively directed by individual combinations of biology, culture, emotions, collective histories, personal experiences and expectations. For example, our hormones are only one factor that directs us to be spellbound by soft curves and thoroughly enchanted by jiggly bits - just as much as we are drawn to clean lines, strength and firm muscles. We are also generally drawn to youthful (but not necessarily 'young'!), symmetrical faces with clear skin indicating general health and wellbeing. Many of us are magnetised to highly distinctive facial and bodily features, others to signs of maturity in search of a sense of stability and wisdom. No one human has ever been nor is, 100% masculine or feminine as we are all elements of both.

There is a kind of 'libido limbo' produced where we are troubled by what we each 'should' look like, act like, be attracted to and enjoy in terms of our sexuality and gender identities. This Anxiety has collectively led to the creation of particular false 'norms' and illusory ideals about our bodies and feelings - that none of us can possibly live up to. Perhaps this is why we project 'approved sexuality' on to celebrities and then uphold their bodies, thoughts and preferences as the new norm? In creating idols to emulate, we detach ourselves from addressing the problem of self-acceptance exactly as we actually are. Ironically though, those idols then become the maintaining force of what is considered good, right and appropriate, even if they represent no-one but themselves.

There is so much secret shaming going on, on a very subtle almost invisible level in our conversations, our language, in entertainment, our memes, jokes and in our products and services - and how they are advertised. A good example of this is where men are criticised by (mostly) women for looking at (other) women's boobs. Contrastingly, women are criticised (very often by other women as well as men) for admiring a man's fancy car or expensive tastes. Of course, this is not confined to XX or XY biology either. So, let me bust a couple of myths here. Those who are drawn to boobs aren't 'perverts' and those drawn to wealth aren't 'shallow'.

Generally speaking (and without going into complex gender politics), psychology suggests that heterosexual men are driven by an unconscious biological drive to seek women who embody certain fertility characteristics that are a physical display of oestrogen such as long, strong hair, nails and curves - namely ample breasts and bums, wide hips and so on (although, these are also determined by other cultural factors too).

Similarly, (generally speaking) many women are impressed by an expensive suit, career success and a big bank balance over any measurement of the body. This is considered to be because our earlier female ancestors relied on attracting a mate who would be able to feed, defend and care for her when pregnant and once her child was born. Put simply, this is evident in the attraction to 'caveman' strength and also more latterly, personal wealth. Either way, this kind of attractiveness is 'social dominance', the ability to protect. Ever wondered why the 'unattractive' but funny guys get dates? They have an ability to influence a room or even stadium - their comedy provides them with incredible social dominance.

The point here is that 'attractiveness' is not as physical as it seems. Those desirable traits on the surface are in many ways an illusion. We are each attracted to indicators of what we need and desire in our lives, not necessarily the actual bodies we see before us. No-one is a 'pervert' or 'deviant' for being drawn to nature, wherever they see beauty and connection. There is no hierarchy of 'correct attractiveness'.

This is why striving to be who we are not or going to great lengths to enhance 'this or that' is almost certain to lead to Anxiety.

Regardless of sexual orientation or gender identity, as humans we are each perfectly entitled to admire another's curves and lines, cars and wit as an expression of shared humanity. There is no 'moralistic' quality to approve or disapprove of.

Anxiety over our attractiveness is largely a fear of being rejected by others on the basis of something we cannot hide or change (although we try) - our bodies, and how we feel about them.

We are all amazing and perfect in our differences and sameness.

We are resplendent creatures featuring a universal variety of ratios and quirks within each of us. We are supposed to be diverse. Human attractiveness is ultimately a state of growth, not fear, so it is in our attitude and our hearts and minds that attraction truly matters.

It is not so much the body itself but our openness to accept ourselves as a perfect reflection of the Universe and to receive one another, just as they are. Attractiveness is not a matter of being seen as looking like so-and-so nor having 'this or that' to show off, but rather it is about one particular proportion - all 100% of YOU. This leads me perfectly on to the ironic issue of perfection-ism...

Perfectionism

Why do we all worry about perfection and presentation? Because we think everyone else is achieving it? Or that despite not being perfect themselves, they will judge imperfection?

Well... if they do, let them. If they are seeking perfection in you... it's because they lack so much more in themselves.

Focus on being REAL. On being exactly who you really ARE. This is TRUTH. Being your own authentic self does not require competition or validation. I for one am happy to never be perfectly presented. I am instead, excited to be a continual work in progress. I am not a finished product. In fact, I would shudder at being considered 'finished' - and up for consumption like a Barbie doll. Real people aren't immaculately presented in boxes, tied in place by the shackles of consumer demand and waiting on the shelf for false liberation in idolatry, because people grow and change.

Seeking Love

As so many of our anxieties are rooted in a fear of being lonely, let's consider this:

In love, never seek someone to be your 'better half' or to 'complete' you - be the whole person you already are. YOU are 'The One'. Only when two whole people come together can lives be truly shared. You both need to have an existing life to share in - not be out to share in someone else's out of a personal lack.

We tend to seek out others romantically with notions of their 'completing us' or being the 'better half... wholeness/ individuality... Ironically, we think we love them but actually it's how they influence how we feel about ourselves that counts. Finding someone with whom we appreciate ourselves better is the aim - not someone with whom we will always feel inadequacy or Anxiety. Or be in search of the 'one' based on criteria that can never be fulfilled.

In order to share a life with another we first need to have one to offer - not assume we will share in theirs and become 'fulfilled'. Two halves don't make a whole. They remain two individual halves forever bargaining and compromising for their own half to be 'completed'.

Instead, be the whole person you already are, and accept that only a complete other is going to be suitable. Otherwise, what is there to share? How can you ever grow?

Unfulfilled people often become resentful of others. In romantic relationships and also, across the board of interaction. Here so many anxieties are provoked by the misplaced judgements and comments of others. Let's consider...

The missing pieces tell an untold story

Romantic relationships, families and friendship groups are like jigsaws. Everyone assumes there is a one overall cohesive picture, made up of the members as combining pieces. but as each member grows and develops, they form their own jigsaw within their piece. When a piece of their jigsaw goes missing, they may no longer fit well in the overall picture.

You may never know why she or he left or fell out with everyone but what you do know is that the jigsaw is always more complex than it seems, and you are missing pieces from your overall understanding. You did not, you do not, and you probably will never find that missing piece and see the overall picture.

Malicious gossip is a bitter pill indeed - but it's only poisonous if you swallow it

Everyone has their reasons, few have an excuse. Observing their reasons - they are unhappy, they fear or resent you, they are in some way injured - helps you to move on from being a victim. You may be a target, but you don't need to be a victim too.

The irony is that it is not just the target who must avoid swallowing the said pill. For gossip to spread and be effective, it needs carriers. Those who spread it are gladly swallowing it whole - and as a result become embroiled in unnecessary unpleasantness. They don't see it, but they too are being poisoned.

Those who spread gossip become the (unwitting perhaps) apathetic foot soldiers of the offender. Offenders rely completely on the gullibility or neediness of apathetic people to do the dirty work for them. It's easy to make such people feel included in a 'secret' or that they themselves are important to have been shared the 'information'. Their egos make them a target. They are being lied to and used - yet they don't see it, perhaps not even until it's too late and their own shame of participation is exposed. They don't realise the irony that in spreading gossip the perpetrator of the gossip does not respect them, in fact they are being used to target someone else of more significance.

It thus becomes easy to spot troublemakers - the initiators and the offenders - as they form a 'circle of sick'. A poisoned well, a murky pool of emotionally sickly people. Such people don't even realise they are being deliberately poisoned. They are kept unaware as they are enjoying the toxin's immediate effects of feeling socially significant.

If you are being bullied (because gossip is bullying), my advice would firstly, to recognise that it's not truthful and that the truth will out to those conscious/smart enough to care.

Secondly, to take all this effort as a back-handed (though back-stabbing) compliment which suggests that you are in fact perceived to be worth the time and effort. You must be a threat or, be holding enviable traits or, are feared to be in the way of some goal or other. i.e. for some reason, you matter more to your bully than all of those muck spreaders put together.

Thirdly, move beyond any involvement - it's poisonous. Don't spend your time in it. Any retaliation or interaction you provide your bully with will be seen as a success for them - and will *encourage* their behaviour. Instead simply share your truth with those who deserve your time.

Remember - bullies want to possess your attention. Don't give it. Don't feed the trolls.

If as in my own experiences, it's a faceless online troll or even a journalist who is targeting you, remember about keeping perspective and that tabloids sell noise - not real 'news'. They are 'noisepapers' which scream at you from the gutter shelf, their aim is to catch attention and invoke fear, scorn or loathing. It is unwise to ever give them your attention.

Often, the biggest weapon a person or organisation wields is simply fear itself. Do you know the origin of the 'laconic phrase'? I love this story. It's a perfect example of why keeping it simple in the face of direct conflict is the best tactic.

The term 'laconic' means to be 'blunt', 'terse' in your speech or 'to the point'. For fellow etymology nerds, the word originates form a place called Laconia in ancient Sparta (Greece).

Here the story tells us that whilst merrily conquering Greece, Philip II of Macedon sent a message to the Spartan military to essentially 'frighten them into submission' without battle by 'asking' whether he should come as *friend or foe'*. The Spartan reply was:

"Neither."

He then sent a more directly threatening message:

"You are advised to submit without further delay, for if I bring my army into your land, I will destroy your farms, slay your people, and raze your city."

The Spartan replied with a single word:

"If."

The emphasis on the one word 'if' is sheer genius. It absolutely summed up the real power in the situation. That Philip was reliant on invoking fear. In highlighting the possibility that Philip might not be victorious as he assumes, the Spartans created doubt in the mighty leader. The upshot was that the invasion never happened.

In this case, turning the certainty into uncertainty with one word was truly a case of the pen being mightier than the sword.

Begrudge the urge to grudge

Holding onto a grudge is a choice. Grudges are not our pain but represent our pain from wounds inflicted or caused by others. They are not the pain itself but act as a screen to hide the raw wounds from our waking consciousness, allowing us to experienced indignation, anger and resentment - instead of the grief or loss we need to process.

By holding a grudge, we are preventing ourselves from healing. Forgiveness is not about the 'other' person, it is about ourselves. To forgive someone is not the same as dismissing or diminishing what they have done, instead it is a process - a process of letting go of the negative effects it maintains on us. Forgiveness releases anger and with it the toxic heat that causes illness in us. It's like if someone were to press a hot coal onto our hand - it would hurt. Now we have a choice, to hold on tight and have it continue to burn us or, to let it go and allow the healing to begin. Which would you choose?

It's often hard to do, so think back to the section on needs and ask yourself if the grudge, the blame or resentment you are holding onto is actually fulfilling or satiating a secret need - maybe it's become part of your social identity? Or being a victim in some way gives a sense of significance or closeness to others? Then, once you identify where that need is, think of other positive ways to meet it so that you can let go of the hurt that is guaranteed to be limiting, not nourishing you.

Letting go of grudges is not a weakness and is also not our dismissal of the significance of our hurt. Quite the contrary, by allowing ourselves to see the true extent of our wounds and heal we are stronger and enlightened by truth.

Often, gossip is manifested in those who suspect a lacking in their own life - but are in denial of needing to work on it. That whatever it is that another has or is doing differently, the real problem is that it highlights the lack of having and doing in the beholder. Because so many of our anxieties are rooted in a fear of failure, let's consider:

Failure IS success

If you really cannot lose then you cannot really win.

How is success measured when you are creating something new? And by whom? Those you have superseded? Those who feel challenged? What are we comparing? All historical heroes have gone AGAINST the status quo, not upheld it in the face of some demon of destruction. Those famous artists whom we celebrate go against the artistic norm of their day but were considered heretical at the time. To rebel is not to sin, it's to challenge their contemporary moral or spiritual boundary.

Often, people become caught up in observing the success that someone else has as though it highlights their own lack. Resentment and jealousy often creep in because there are unhelpful thoughts arising that suggest that 'if she is having more success than me, then there is less for me to have'. Now let's just explode that myth right now. Success is not a finite resource. Like creativity, the more you or anyone else has, the more it generates. If someone gets 5 minutes of fame in a particular genre, it increases public awareness of that whole genre. If someone gets a promotion in a company it means that company is doing well and likely to expand.

Furthermore, if someone gets the lead role in a show or wins that competition we were hoping to win, then be reassured that it was not because of some 'lack' on our part. Instead it is simply that the other person was 'more right' at that particular time under the particular mass of circumstances (which are so multitudinous we could never fathom them all.

Now it's not just about being magnanimous and 'happy for others', there is a subtle yet powerful ironic direct benefit you can choose to have. When we credit others, we credit ourselves. When we celebrate the wins and highs of others, we invite ourselves to share in that win too. There is no failure in celebrating the win. Wins are not exclusive.

If you are insisting on thinking that you actually *cannot* do a certain thing then what you are really doing is *avoidance* behaviour. You are imposing self-limiting beliefs that justify your not trying. This is one way in which self-belief is the foundation of manifesting reality.

So, when you notice the thought 'I cannot' remember that this also means the polar opposite might also be true. Focus on the 'I can' and then take it even further and say: 'I am'. This way your thoughts are directing creative force - a will to accomplish. Your thoughts will manifest the CAN DO rather than the cannot.

When we try something and don't succeed the first time, this does not mean the 'can do' thought was wrong - it is your assumption that everything must happen the first time it is tried, that is wrong.

How often do you notice that when you physically reach for something just beyond your grasp, it only takes another one or two attempts to reach it? Show a toddler a biscuit an inch too far away and you'll see the magic.

"Whether you think you can, or you think you can't - you're right."
Henry Ford

So 'failure' doesn't actually exist as a 'thing' - what you perceive as failure is just the pathway to success. It's the tries. It's the effort. It's the faith. Again, we come back to faith and doubt being the same thing - you can only have faith IF you can have doubt.

Think back to a time when you kept trying at something. Maybe it's lifting a certain weight or getting a poem published or passing your driving test. You wouldn't have made that second, third or hundredth attempt unless the faith was already there. You wouldn't have made that first doubtful try if you didn't know you could and would (eventually) succeed.

The trick is to hold the positive thought, allow yourself to feel the positive emotions associated with having ALREADY SUCCEEDED, and 'move into' that mind space of belief. The body will follow suit and manifest the reality. Aligning your thoughts with the corresponding emotions allows you step into a belief. It is that 'belief' that then pulls you forward into making that reality happen.

Feeling like a fraud?

It's common to hold back on success and growth because of something known as 'Imposter Syndrome'. Imposter Syndrome is when a person feels inadequate despite being highly qualified in their expertise and experience. They feel overwhelmed by the feeling that they do not know enough to be called an 'expert' or 'leader' in their field and *will ultimately* be exposed as a *fraud*, or *imposter*.

There is, I think, a kind of ironic truism in here that I believe is experienced: *the more you know about something, the more you realise that you know almost nothing!*

> *"I never am really satisfied that I understand anything;
> because, understand well as I may, my comprehension can only
> be an infinitesimal fraction of all I want to understand about
> the many connections and relations which occur to me."*
> **Ada Lovelace**

In recognising that you are experiencing this, take comfort in that ironically, *feeling like a fraud* because you just don't know enough suggests that you value integrity - and are in a genuine position of having tremendous insight. So much so, that you realise the magnitude and sheer scope of your genre. A deluded foozler wouldn't be experiencing that sense of scale.

The upshot is that feeling like a fraud holds you back. It means that you halt, or limit, your personal development, your work, your happiness - the wider development of your reality and your contribution to the world.

So, what can you do about it? Well, it all begins with asking *'what if...?'*

What if you are only one step away from curing the common cold? Or two articles away from a great publishing deal? What if you are holding back not only yourself but how you might be facilitating your team winning? Or playing your special role in a radical, industrial change for a cleaner Earth? Or leading by example in a joyful social movement that calls for your authenticity? What if...?

With so much potential at stake, it's important to understand what beliefs are preventing you from progress - from taking positive risks on yourself. In this often-crippling place of self-doubt, we have to contend with the fear of not being 'enough', but there is often a further miscalculation also going on - regarding the level of knowledge of others. There is a de-valuing of the self and simultaneously, an *over*-valuing of others when you assume others to be far more clued up than they actually are. Often because they simply say they are.

One of the most confounding factors of this is when your area of interest becomes trendy and/or profitable. In such a situation there is often a sudden emergence of many 'experts' - whom you don't recognise nor relate to. This is especially true online where there is unlimited space for grandstanding and let's be brutally honest, it's easy to get away with dishonesty.

So, let's travel a little further along this self-esteem steam train because it's important to recognise that not everyone who claims to be an expert is any such thing.

In contrast to Imposter Syndrome there is the Dunning-Kruger effect (named after two psychologists, Dunning and Kruger, whose work on cognitive bias and the role of self-awareness in incompetence goes back to the 90s). This is where a person with a little knowledge, insight or ability in something vastly over-estimates their expertise or abilities. This is not just about how they present themselves to others - it's a genuine belief they hold about themselves too. These 'experts' lack that same self-awareness that Imposter Syndrome experiencers are wrestling with. Therefore, they are more likely to be online making false claims, confusing the public and unwittingly undermining the real experts. Not only are they likely to be assertive in sharing their 'expert' status, they believe it too.

The Dunning-Kruger effect is all about a LACK of self-awareness, so someone exhibiting this effect is unlikely to be genuinely doubting themselves - and would not suspect an over-estimation in themselves. When so many ultra-confident experts you've never heard of are all telling you how amazing they are, it's easy to believe it. Especially when it is a repeating message and confirms your emotional reasoning of self-doubt. It's so easy to feel that you simply don't belong to the identity of the (fake) expertise because you don't identify with it.

As an anxious person I have often worried that I exhibit the Dunning-Kruger effect. In fact, it held up the release of this book. But of course, I realised the fundamental irony: if I was indeed a 'DK doofus', I wouldn't be experiencing the self-doubt and limiting my output. I simply wouldn't be having this conversation with myself. It is in the Anxiety itself that I can be reassured that this worry is misplaced. In noticing this, I have learned to take any worries that I'm a DK doofus as a sign of Imposter Syndrome at work!

Imposter Syndrome is likely to be quietly, even secretly experienced. It would show in behaviours and thoughts such as hesitation to engage with others or take opportunities, procrastination around releasing work, critical tone of self-talk and avoidance of criticism (like compulsive editing and re-editing and re-re-editing...).

So, if you are noticing that you are not moving forward in your career and you recognise signs of Anxiety like hesitation, procrastination, critical tone of self-talk, avoidance, compulsive editing and re-editing and a burning fear of being 'found out' for not being the expert that *'you think everyone thinks you think you are'*, despite a history of relevant expertise and experience, then there is a good chance that Imposter Syndrome has taken hold.

IS or BS? How to manage your experience...

Firstly, accept that your self-doubt is a wayward sign of your ever-growing insight and integrity. It is Anxiety reminding you of your values.

Secondly, let go of the word 'expert' (or similar). You don't need it. No-one actually does. There is no need to claim to be an expert. Other people will do that. Cite your own journey, your mission, your history, your trials, your misses, your successes, your aims - that's your personal truth and it isn't up for debate. If your work is good then your results speak for you. Let go of the attachment to the identity. Let the ego take a nap - you don't need approval or permission from anyone to do what you do. Move forward and upwards as you embrace the wealth of learning and the joy of experience that is always before you, as well as behind you.

Furthermore, there is way too much importance placed on the word 'expert'. What does 'expert' even mean? Academic? Field experience? Customer success? Money earned? Money invested? Press interest? Peer approval? Years spent? Number of certificates? Number of accolades (and who accredits these bodies to give the awards anyway)? There are lots of great ideas about expertise - like Malcom Gladwell's 10,000 hours of practice rule (see his excellent book 'Outliers') - but there is no precise meaningful definition that can be uniformly applied across industries and genres. Furthermore, I often wonder how specific we need to be, to be an 'expert'? Can a person be an expert in something new or does expert status only come when there is something to compare to? What about people like me who have a 'portfolio career' spanning different and contrasting areas rather than one?

The main point here is that all the uncertainty and ambiguity of what it means to be an expert is why we have a problem. The vague sense of what it means and the incongruency of application provides fertile ground for Impostor Syndrome to take hold and choke genuine progress whilst simultaneously creating room for the Dunning-Kruger Effect to grow. This is why that feeling of being 'enough' is so damn elusive - at least it is to those who care about it.

Thirdly, look to how people around you respond to your work. No-one you genuinely respect and look up to would be supporting you in your genre nor others trying to join you where you are right now, if you were indeed an imposter or fraud or doofus. If you respect these people, then trust that they would spot a true imposter. Uphold your respect for *them* by accepting their respect for *you*. This comes down not so much to how good you are at rating yourself, but rather rating your peers and contemporaries as people you aspire to belong with. The people around you, reflect you.

Lastly, recognise that not everyone who says they are an expert knows what they are talking about. Over-valuing others' expertise (and down-grading your own) is very easy when you feel confused as to who they are and you're averse to competing in a contest you didn't sign up for. Try not be overwhelmed by the (false) appearance of so many 'experts' online. Take it as a sign that what you have been authentically involved with has grown in interest and therefore this is YOUR time to shine.

Remember too that after all is said and done, it's the innovators and adapters who make progress - after the repeaters are worn out and redundant. It is in being bold and daring that growth occurs. Being an 'expert' on the status quo is only useful if you plan to break it.

Is there a doctor on board? Yes - it's you!

Our thoughts and emotions have an enormous impact on our wellbeing. We know that the mind-body connection is fundamental to how Anxiety operates and is maintained and now we can look at the bigger picture on all areas of our health and illness.

Not only our mental wellbeing but our biology too. The most recent areas of scientific research are astonishing in demonstrating how we can heal our bodies by the intention of our minds. This is not wishful thinking - it is science. It is also ironically 'wish *fulfilment*' where we manifest our health (good health and illnesses too). The cutting edge culture of scientific healing research is upholding so much of what our ancient ancestors 'knew' (albeit in a different sense of understanding).

For example, the field of 'psychoneuroimmunology' demonstrates that our immune systems are affected by our thoughts, feelings and beliefs. Recovery from other types of illness including the complete remissions of tumours and other serious terminal illnesses have been repeatedly shown to be linked to *belief or disbelief in the efficacy of a treatment.*

Pain and irritation do not actually 'occur' at the site of the problem - the pain and irritation is actually occurring in the brain and we experience it as though it is located elsewhere. Think about having an itchy nostril and you will create that experience. Do it! See how quickly you need to scratch - even though you know there is no irritant there, it was merely a suggestion you made to yourself. Think about biting really hard into a big juicy lemon... NOM-NOMmmmm... Are you wincing at all? Salivating? Now try to tell me there is no immediate direct mind-body biological influence.

Having followed placebo research for nearly 20 years now with utter fascination, I'm a crazy fanatic for its results and its further potential in not only physical healing but also emotional and psychological healing... and the bigger overall picture of collective healing across our planet and beyond. In the later chapter on IFFY Practice, I will show you exercises to harness this. Anxiety occurs whether the threat is really 'out there' or in our minds, and yet we experience very real physical results (both biological and behavioural). Here we can see how it's all too easy to create our own illnesses and limitations and yet, if we transmute our experiences for good, we can achieve the opposite.

Some of the most fascinating current material comes from neuropsychologist Dr. Mario Martinez who talks about 'archetypal wounds'. He posits that 'shame, abandonment and betrayal' lead to embodied illness, for example, shame is experienced as 'heat' and causes inflammation leading to illnesses such as fibromyalgia.

Similarly, neuroscientist Dr. Joe Dispenza (who has written numerous books on how to elicit the 'placebo response' inside yourself) and other major proponents such as Dr. Bruce Lipton are in the astonishing field of epigenetics. Epigenetic research shows how our genes are affected by our environment and, that genetic expressions can be switched on or off in response to what's going around us. Crucially, as with the Anxiety - it's not limited to what is occurring or changing around us, but also the environment we create *within* our minds.

Harnessing the power of belief, this field shows us that since our biology is instructed to change and adapt by environment, it doesn't have to be the environment 'out there'. We can change from within because belief is what creates our experience of reality. The body doesn't perceive a difference between the two, it responds to the one we choose.

As mind-blowingly modern as this all sounds, it's quite possibly the oldest trick in the medical textbooks. I'm going to offer a bit more background information on all of this as it is so important to appreciate just how fundamentally ironic all of this is when we consider the typical outlook on how to 'manage symptoms' largely ignores the basic premise of mind-body influence - and its massive potential for good.

From sacred medicine-men and holy shrines; to the strange charms, rituals and magic potions of the intellectually and socially peculiar groups who tend to dress in white. That is both of the past, and today where our high-status members of academia are stereotyped in lab-coats and have a very complex language, understood only by the rightfully initiated. The cross-over of paradigms in healing, old and new, that co-exist today are often at times methodologically and theoretically conflicting; from modern conventional prescriptive medicines and psychological treatments to ancient 'complementary therapies' such as acupuncture and reflexology.

There is a large devotion to various forms of a more spiritual healing such as faith healing, crystal healing and prayer. Although many of the old, bizarre and potentially damaging methods such as ingestion of frogs-sperm, monkey dung, and ground bones; or cutting, bleeding and blistering; or shocking/freezing and even bludgeoning; are no longer used, many old and new methods are still sought and relied upon. The one thing that links them in common with one another is that they are all regularly associated with illness and are (or were) at one point believed to heal. The one thing that has been guaranteed consistent over time; endured all the scrutiny of every new medical fad and idea; is that by some means, people tend to get better.

The number of remedies long forgotten and those still used today that have relied solely on the placebo effect is astounding and equally frightening; the US office of Technology have estimated that of the modern medicine readily available, only 1 in 5 has been proven to have any pharmacological effect; in fact to some degree all of them have a reliance on the placebo effect! The terms 'placebo' and 'placebo effect' were first introduced into the language of physicians in 1811 via publication of a new medical dictionary - where the placebo effect was believed to be a treatment given to the patients to please them rather than medicate them; to 'cheer the spirits'. The mysterious, latent power behind the placebo lay unrecognised and ignored by most for over a century.

The term 'placebo' is Latin for 'I will please' and has been a universal medical mystery for as long as cures for sickness have been sought. Clearly many a charlatan has relied upon the placebo effect for sales, perhaps even innocently so. Of course, the placebo effect does have a harmful alter-ego, the Nocebo Effect. This is the polar opposite of such a healing mechanism and translates as 'I will harm'. This is essentially how curses work - someone receives the 'curse', believes it so and therefore manifests the experience of it.

Recent interest in what we now term psychosomatic illness and areas of health psychology where the immunosuppressive effects of grief are studied demonstrate this universal self-harming phenomenon and have resulted in the beginning of a paradigm shift in western medical thinking.

It is important to note that the placebo effect, which is one of healing or relief from symptoms, is not caused, per se. by the administered placebo. It cannot be. A placebo is inert by definition and so it seems that it is in the action of taking the placebo that results in the effect. The explanations behind the placebo effect are thought to apply to the nocebo effect too, as both phenomena are thought to be two ends of the same spectrum. The placebo effect has been rarely studied in its own right until recently through the emergence of new fields not directed by pharmacological interests. This is often because placebo effects are treated as a nuisance variable in clinical trials and attempts are generally made to control it, rather than explore it.

Although current ethical restrictions prevent 'Sham' operations from being carried out (phew! That's a worry you didn't need to collect!), they were done in the past, some within the past seventy years. A sham operation is where subjects were anaesthetised and an incision made - but closed up without the surgical intervention. Knee operations and heart surgery (!) are among some of the studies showing that 'sham operations' did lead to great relief in some people, with some actually improving in say, heart function.

The role of expectancy is very important. As there is no particular placebo-prone personality, the psychological make-up of the individual patient has next to no effect on the outcome of a placebo response. In contrast however, the attitude, behaviour and contextual knowledge of the medical practitioner seems to also be very important in determining a positive response in a patient's health.

Similarly, as discussed previously, the power of ritual is massively overlooked and undermined by assertions that 'proper science' dismisses ritual as 'superstitious behaviour'. For example, in obsessive-compulsive disorder, anxious thoughts are 'neutralised' by a person's personal compulsions (rituals like hand washing, tapping their fingers or safety checking). These are ritualised actions which therapists will actively discourage in an attempt to break the vicious cycle, by cessation of the compulsion.

Now, we know that in performing such rituals in response to worries, we actually reinforce the worry - and so it's unhelpful as a strategy long-term (even though it feels as though it works in the moment). This is why the strategy becomes disordered.

However, it may seem counter-intuitive to therefore regard ritual as useful, but it is the direction and intention for which it is used that renders it useful or harmful. Again, we see where an effective mind-body link is dismissed when instead it could be flipped and used to manifest growth and progression. Eons of spirituality attest to the positive power of ritual where acts such as dressing in a certain way, chanting mantras, lighting candles, praying/meditation, drawing or creating art in specific ways are effective as both therapeutic and spiritual practices. Similarly, we see this positive manifesting occur through ritual where top athletes or performing artists may schedule time for their mantras, be wearing their 'lucky underpants' or have pre-show self-care routines that enable them to become highly focused on their wins and visualise their intended performance outcomes.

The implications of the placebo effect stretch to every corner of medicine and health care. The idea that sad people prefer yellow pills to blue ones; that branded tablets work better than unfamiliar ones but two unbranded placebos work better than one; that some therapies 'work better' in some cultures over others and that when the doctor says 'take two paracetamol and call me in the morning...' a strange and complex formulae to wellbeing emerges.

Although the administration of a placebo implies it to be a chemically inert substance, it seems that the form i.e. colour, size and shape or that the attitude and belief of doctors and patients are far from inert. This 'power' of suggestion certainly gives rise to endless possibilities of how our individual and societal well-being could be influenced and affected by our culture, lifestyles and technology; not to mention the implications of the power of advertising and media.

A world where medical attention could be concentrated on the seriously ill and helpless while others harness their natural abilities to heal minor and common complaints sounds like it would result in more productive day-to-day lives for everyone with less sick days taken and less hospital beds occupied. What are the limitations to self-healing and the physical influence of the mind? Are there any?

Perhaps the manufacturers of 'tic-tacs' could employ a whole new marketing strategy and sell yellow coloured, 'pick-me-up' breath fresheners that keep both your breath and brain fresh at the mere cost of a mint.

Furthermore, if we are to uncover more of the mechanisms behind self-healing, then perhaps we could further understand why we get sick in the first place and dare to prevent the development of disease. After all, prevention is better than a cure and it all starts with how we choose to think and feel.

For many of us our anxieties are rooted in existential questions about the nature of being and god-stuff, so let's consider:

In the beginning there was the word, and the word was "Go..."

'Creation' is a much argued about and highly emotionally charged subject. In the West it is curiously based around whether we subscribe to one theory *or* another... e.g. the 'big bang' *or* the 7 days of biblical Genesis, but the problem here lies in assuming that creation itself was a singular event that *happened*, that it is somehow confined to one moment in the past - that it was a single completed event.

No matter how far back in time we go to try and explain how something 'began', there is always something even earlier to explain. It is truly the biggest 'whodunit' mystery ever written.

For example, if God 'did it' just before having a Sunday rest, where did He/She/They get their supplies and slippers from? If the big bang is responsible, then how did it come about? In what state, place, or dimension were those chemical elements suspended on the run up to the noisy start of our Universe? Neither of these lines of historical enquiry are particularly helpful as they lead to more questions, anchored in the concept of historic time.

If we consider instead that creation is in the NOW that it is ongoing, that we ARE it happening back then, now and tomorrow, then these arguments become redundant (although they remain fascinating).

We are constantly creating ourselves, literally. From general procreation and birth of our own species (directly from our own cells, our energy or life force and our mind-boggling DNA blueprints) to the day to day, minute to minute personal interactions we have with each other and the world we inhabit.

We are constantly thinking and doing, acting and reacting. We are in a *process* of creation with each other and all that our universe holds, including the perceived empty space (which I think of as holding 'potential').

From looking at the trees and hearing the birds sing and chatter, to smelling the salt in sea air and tasting our coffee in the morning as the sun glimmers upon the surface of our worldly surroundings and illuminates our senses. As we interact with each other we motivate, challenge (and even create blocks or difficulties as well as opportunities). In all of this we are in the act of creating.

As we breathe, we literally create, destroy, and create anew, in an eternal cycle. When we breathe in, we 'in-spire' (draw new) and when we then breathe out, we 'ex-pire' (transform). Just by waking and breathing each day, we are creating our own existence, together. Feeling *inspired* yet?

Where we begin to (or increasingly) apply our conscious self-awareness of this act of collaborative creation and all that follows, we can begin to appreciate the sheer magnitude of our minds' capabilities (even in the smallest tasks), we also begin to see the 'divine spark' that is in each of us.

(As a side note, this is why I am always happy to see and accept a dishevelled and unpreened self, to not spend all of my time seeking physical acceptance or 'perfection'. I will never be perfectly presented because I am not a finished product. I am still in the act of creation.)

So in summary, when creation begun, (assuming there was a beginning) and however you 'storyboard' the event that essentially brought 'nothingness into somethingness' whether from unconscious cosmic disruption or from some intelligent source, the only thing that was needed was inertia - some kind of intention to create. I believe that this is where it all began - with the word 'Go'.

What is 'go'? Well, put simply 'go' is what happens when intention meets action, giving rise to what we experience as Conscious Awareness.

One of the more abstract thoughts I've carried since my earliest ponderings of The Big Questions, is that if it were at all possible to encapsulate the ineffable, then the name of God will likely be best penned as a ridiculously simple mathematical equation. Whether you call it God, Source, the Universe, The All... I call it 'Potential'. Infinite Potential...

Maybe instead of a massively complicated equation with 20,000 volumes of proof, maybe the symbol that is the name of God almighty would simply turn out as smiley emoji: 😊

But why do bad things happen to good people? A quandary often felt by those seeking answers to the Big Questions. Let's consider:

Coping with 'bad things happening', general state of the world...

Because so much of our Anxiety is tied up in fears about loss, injustice, unfairness, we need to get a handle on accepting that bad things happen.

Why do bad things happen to good people? The reason is that bad things happen because all things are possible. Similarly good things happen to 'bad' people!

Ultimately all these worries actually boil down to one underlying worry - 'I won't cope'. For example:

"If I lost my job I won't be able to pay my mortgage and I'll lose the house and I won't be able to get another job paying enough and I'll be homeless and... I... won't cope."

"If she doesn't accept me then I must be unlovable and I will be lonely forever and I will live alone - and I will not cope... and I will die (alone)."

But ironically, things that happen are actually neither good nor bad. They are emotionally neutral. The good or bad is subjective and occurs within us - as our emotional experience of those events. The events themselves don't hold any emotion - it's us that do.

Sadness, anger, grief, fear are not to be seen as 'bad' things. They are uncomfortable and even unbearable to us as the experiencers, however, they occur because we have the equal and opposite capacity for joy, love, fulfilment and freedom. It is in our pain that we actually grow. If we never struggle then we never reach beyond what we already can do.

Whatever the event or experience brings, we can always know

that it also marks 'change'. How we change is up to us and the decisions we then make.

In our sense of loss we can come to realise our sense of connectedness. That when we are alone we are at our most interconnected, undistracted from the mental work of categorising and interpreting the world into illusions.

On the matter of death itself, here we see an enormous irony. After a lifetime of changing on a daily basis, death is the ultimate physical change we undergo. We return to the stardust and starlight from whence we came. Nothing is 'destroyed' except the ego - the illusion of the self. All matter and energy are transformed. If there was no ego trying to hold it all together, there would be no fear of death at all.

Yet, we are consumed with terror by this apparent cessation of being as though we fall into some 'dark abyss'. But a dark abyss is simply a place of space - a gap full of potential and understanding, if only we could shine some light into it. We can.

My beautiful religious renegade friend, Rev. Michael Hampson, put it like this in his book *God Without God:*

> *"The end is a mystery, but so was the beginning.*
> *To the mystery of the beginning we first ascribed the name*
> *Existence of Being, and then, with due caution, the name God.*
> *The end is the same mystery. We return to that mystery.*
> *We return to God, whatever we have imagined that to be:*
> *the dust of the ground, or the atmosphere, or the mystery*
> *at the heart of existence itself."*
> **Rev. Michael Hampson**

Crises are opportunities

Avoiding doing things relates to avoidance of crisis. Anxiety pretty much always boils right down to the assertion or belief that 'I won't cope' in a particular crisis. Remembering too, the fact that you are living in a projected hypothetical future or even re-imagined past really throws a curve-ball on this assertion. However, fear of crisis grips fast and is very hard to shake.

So, think about that fear that is gripping hold of you - is it in the past? Present? Future? If it is in the present, are you dealing with it now? By reading this and other material? If so, then you are already coping marvellously. Give yourself some extra credit!

You see, the fundamental irony in all this is that if we are anxious by nature then we are actually better prepared in any crisis. If that 'thing' ever should occur in any form, be proactively pleased that it will also be your time to SHINE. For example, I'm writing this paragraph during the UK 'Lockdown' in the Coronavirus pandemic... and I've never felt busier or more focused!

Next time you project to a crisis that isn't actually happening, remind yourself that you've already done the mental preparation homework in full technicolour action movie style - and you can give yourself permission to do something else, ideally something calming and pleasant - maybe even go eat a biscuit and watch cartoons :)

Acknowledge your super ability for imagining the worst, the many strategic options and calamitous possibilities that it would bring, then congratulate yourself on your resilience and imagination - and give yourself permission to chill now. As Roman leader Marcus Aurelius kindly reminds us:

"Never let the future disturb you. You will meet it,
if you have to, with the same weapons of reason which
today arm you against the present."
Marcus Aurelius

And this guy is reminding us from the PAST, nearly 2 millennia ago when he ruled the Roman Empire which was constantly at war. Maybe take it on board for today?

Now with all those hypothetical crises averted, give yourself permission to step forward on your journey.

How far to... Enlightenment?

Enlightenment comes not after the accumulation of lots of knowledge but after much contemplation of our thoughts and the eventual abandoning of all thought - surrendering to the mystery. But... is that not the same as not bothering to think at all? It's a journey where the destination is in illusion because each step is the prize, each step is your destiny unfolding.

The length of the journey, the number of steps does not quantify enlightenment in an accumulative way - you don't become more enlightened by adding a mile on or lose a bit by finding a shortcut.

It's all about the quality of your awareness, the abandonment of judgement by the depth of your surrender, the expansion of your consciousness in any given moment so that you might come to experience the Unity of all things. You become one with the universe and therefore, all possible Anxiety dissolves.

Unity is divided!?

Ironically, of course unity is curiously divided too. There is a strange illusion of duality that makes up our understanding of things in balance, harmony, contrast and complement. Think too about all the Hermetic Principles and we see again how clear it is that our experience of life is fundamentally paradoxical. In order to experience Unity there must be possible division of parts. Remembering that the 'gap' the perceived nothingness is not empty? The gap is full of potential. In fact, the Kabbalah refers to an 'infinite nothingness' from which even our fundamental notion of god comes.

Have you ever looked at a Moebius strip? It's one continuous strip with a single half-twist in it, and the two ends connected. You can make these with a strip of paper and a glue stick. It provides an illusion of two sides and yet when you run a little critter across its surface it would take one complete journey across both sides, without ever crossing a 'boundary'.

Similarly, in the Chinese Taoist 'Yin and Yang' symbol of dualistic balance, it is not possible to draw one without drawing the other.

So, separation is an illusion. In our modern times of polarised thinking, it is no surprise that we live in a state of Anxiety over what to think and believe. Similarly, science and religion are both thought of as seeking truth, but this is misleading as it implies that there is some 'one truth' to be got at and had.

> *"Truth is one; sages call it by various names."*
> **The Rig Veda**

Instead they are modalities of seeking understanding and ultimately a feeling of belonging in this universe. They are motivated by the same questions, the same 'quest', if you like. They are both journeys, but they take different paths and count different milestones. They perceive different kinds of danger and threat, different forms of obstruction and darkness along the way. They see each other through cultural and philosophical lenses and therefore, perceive adversary in their difference.

IF - Ironic Fundamentalism

CHAPTER FOUR

IFFY PRACTICE FOR MANIFESTING YOUR ATARAXIA

Finding the IF is a daily practice of asking 'What If...?' questions, of 're-wiring' yourself for positivity by forging new neural pathways inside, new adventures outside and by noticing and utilising the ironic wisdom around you. Here are some suggestions:

- Affirmations, mantras and rituals to focus you on your positive direction of growth.

- Creative ironic projects in your home as a constant source of inspiration e.g. curate interesting art, curiosities, little collections of fun things...

- Create vision boards of what you actually DO want in life, and not things you don't want.

- Enjoy the arts that make you think e.g. satire, comedy, burlesque etc.

- Enjoy learning about the changes and innovation in science and technology. If you understand how it all works and why it makes it easy to not feel 'left behind' and yet also not 'feel obliged to participate'.

- Listen to others you find strange and just hear them, try to see their points of view, with suspended judgement. This doesn't mean you have to agree with them!

- Imagine enjoying contrary and opposite scenarios to those you are used to. Maybe you are a carnivore that might like to try going veggie?

- Try to actively 'like' the things you avoid - just to see what that looks and feels like.

- Take positive risks and try new things.

- Notice when counter intuition is trying to stop you - and laugh while ignoring it.

All we know is that we do not really 'know' anything - because there are no certainties. We are always looking through a lens, subject to bias, challenged by our own perspective. We create our realities. Our experiences and expectations shape our emerging, ever-morphing realities and they exist entangled with our experience of it.

So being in a state of Anxiety typically means to have an inability to tolerate uncertainty. So, we have a choice. We can take our multifaceted individual experience of Anxiety (its physical symptoms, thoughts, feelings and behaviours) and either:

- Continue to be weighed down, held back, kept in a state of fear and inability to move forward.

or

- We can drop the negative judgement of Anxiety as 'bad' and instead transmute the constituent parts into information, drive, personal power.

Here is how to do it in 3 distinct movements.

The Alchemy of Anxiety

Thinking back on all that we have explored, it's now time to pull it all together, to embrace the paradoxes and resolve them within ourselves. I've summarised the process here for you, it's in three handy parts. To aid you further in this process, I also provide a series of exercises that you can use to help you transmute the experience of Anxiety into personal power for manifesting your best and most fulfilling life.

It's all about attention and intention. Where you place your attention, the direction of that attention and, your intended outcome of your practice. It's time to get clarity on your inner vision of yourself and outer bigger vision *for* yourself - so that both your attention and intention work in alignment to create your happiest and most fulfilling life.

Part 1 - Identify the Anxiety within you

How does anxiety manifest for you?

Physical Sensations:
What does it feel like?
Where in your body do you feel it?

Cognitions:
What do the thoughts sound/look like in your head?
What is the tone?
What are they saying to/about you?

Emotions:

What are you feeling?

Where in the body are you feeling it?

What physical sensations, thoughts and actions is it prompting?

Behaviour:

What unhelpful things are you doing?

What are you not doing that you used to?

Part 2 - Think/feel again...

Being able to use and to hold as many different perspectives at the same time leads to the surrendering of bias. Bias is the ego's defence system; where ego is a kind of operating illusion of our 'fixed identity'.

It is held fast by assumptions so as to avoid being compromised and dissolved. The irony is that ego tries to 'preserve' us by ultimately limiting our perception - and potential to grow.

Similarly, people often think of paradoxes ('non-concordance') as a problem to be solved but instead, ironically, they should be embraced as making perfect sense.

Remember, all paradoxes can be resolved - they can be resolved because we can resolve them. We are the active creative agent who is experiencing them as they occur, so of course we can.

What IF you could transmute Anxiety into personal power?
- *What would that look like?*
- *What would that feel like? (and where do you feel it in your body?)*

- *What thoughts are there?*
- *What action would you now be doing/not doing?*

Compare the 'Whats' and consider how your:

- *Physical sensations reveal* **excitement** *in your body.*
- *Fearful thoughts reveal* **desires** *in your mind.*
- *Emotions reveal* **core values** *from your spiritual self or essence.*
- *Behaviour reveals where you are* **self-limiting and self-sabotaging.**

Consider:

- *Instead of assuming Anxiety, what might you be excited about? Where in the body do you feel it? Which chakra does this relate to?*
- *Are you holding both extremes of thought, the 'this or that' and all the paradoxical possibilities as possible (and not just the first one that popped into your head)? Are you doing this* **without judgement?**
- *What is the emotional reaction telling you about your core values, your true desires?*
- *What is it telling you about your best course of action? What do you need to do/no longer need to do?*

Consider further...

- *How are you getting in your own way?*
- *How can you get out of your own way?*

Part 3 - Choose.

That's it - *choose.*

If you don't know where you are going, you are going the right way.

Now it's time to upgrade that holistic conscious experience, entirely. It is time to put all that practical metaphysics stuff into use.

This is where you can really take all that your Anxiety has taught you through your whole life, transmute the weight of your experience into a force at your back, ready to thrust you forward.

Having a definitive plan as to where exactly you are going is unhelpful. If you knew where you were going to end up, then there would be no real adventure, nor growth.

Furthermore, since expectations are based on assumptions, holding on to expectations of your destiny only sets you up for confusion, distraction, disappointment and... downward Anxiety spirals.

Be careful what you wish for...

As we know very well, there doesn't need to be a 'real' tiger 'out there' to trigger very real physical reactions. This is because the mind does not differentiate between a 'real' and imagined stimulus.

When Hermetically speaking, there is no difference - an imagined apple exists somewhere because all apples are possible, and time and space are an illusion.

An imagined ideal YOU is just as real as the one sitting there doing the imagining. You just need to create that YOU in your mind - and *step into it* as though it is already real in the here and now. Feel it to be true.

Turn that potential you in to the 'real' YOU. Choose it.

This is how top athletes visualise and manifest their wins.

This is how highly successfully entrepreneurs and artists get to the 'top'.

This is how autonomic healing works.

This is what the enormously growing trend for 'manifesting' is all about. Devotees and modern mystics across the globe are investing enormous amounts of money, time and effort in this concept.

This is your time to get rather excited. If you have an anxious disposition, you are actually sitting on a proverbial goldmine of advantage. You are already a pro at this. **You are just used to doing it the other way around.**

Draw on the paradox. Use your creative, imaginative mind - the same one that literally manifests that physical, biological reality of anxiety - *to your advantage instead.*

Rather than focusing on the negative experiences and cycles - deliberately conjure in the mind those thoughts for feeling good, well, successful and happy - and instead these ones will be made *manifest.*

It is that simple. It does take effort - effort called *practice.*

You can choose this.

The IF Exercises

Remember Captain Anxiety? Here are some exercises to supercharge your new superpowers...

EXERCISE 1 - 'Time and Space'
(breathing and relaxation)

This will actually create space and time in which to manifest and invite your thoughts, (including the anxious ones if they appear).

To seriously calm your whole system and relax, I like to use a technique called 'breathing down'. This is a brilliant hack for interrupting panic too. All you do is breathe in through your nose for a count of e.g. 3 counts then breath out longer through your mouth e.g. for 4 counts, in a nice slow rhythm. Completely fill and empty your lungs as you go.

The number of counts doesn't matter too much - as long as you are breathing out for longer than you breathing in. Whatever rhythm works for you is what works for you.

The shorter in breath vs longer out breath is helping to adjust the ratio of oxygen in your body so that your nervous system calms. It's the opposite of 'hyperventilating' - where we rapidly over-breathe and take in more oxygen than we need sending us into panic.

Once you are calm and relaxed, keep your attention anchored on your breath or the rising and falling of your chest or abdomen.

Allow yourself to simply 'notice' any thoughts or sensations without judging or interpreting them.

Are thoughts distracting you? Judgements creeping in?

That's ok. The fact you have noticed means you are acing this. Thank your mind for noticing and return to your anchor (breathing).

Follow with...

EXERCISE 2 - 'Mind the Gap'
(mindfulness meditation on unity)

Allow those thoughts to drift in and off again, like clouds above you and begin to notice the spaces between them.

Focus gently, on the gaps.

If this is tricky, perhaps try listening to a metronome... tick, tick, tick...

Then try to place your attention into the spaces between the ticks - the silences.)

Focus on the gaps.

Keep returning your attention to the gaps. In the gaps there is all the potential.

Follow with...

Now that you can focus on the gaps between the thoughts... it's time to extend those gaps to include all of that 'empty space' too. The space between all the 'stuff' in the universe and all the space between all of the tiny bits of stardust that make you up.

Focus on all those spaces, those gaps, those potentials that reach within you and out from you across the whole Universe.

You are connected by the gaps - united by all the space. Gently allow yourself to be suspended here in all of that potential, in the present moment now.

Remember:
NOTICE ANY FEELINGS OR PHYSICAL SENSATIONS
THAT ARISE - WITHOUT JUDGEMENT

If needed, follow with...

EXERCISE 3 - 'Dial it Down'
(pain, itch, interruption control)

Here, if any sensations are interrupting your focus, again notice them and allow them to move away from your body. Out-with and beyond - to dissolve into all that 'space' you are united with. Consider too that all sensations aren't actually really 'there'- they are occurring in your neurology and are *experienced* as though they are 'there'.

Imagine a dial that controls intensity and see it turn as you 'turn down' the experience. Do it in little increments and notice it work. Keep 'dialling down' and until you can relax again into your gentle focus.

Remember:
NOTICE ANY THOUGHTS THAT ARISE
- WITHOUT JUDGEMENT

If your thoughts are negative... Follow with Exercise 4 and/or 5.

If they are already only positive, skip to Exercise 6!

EXERCISE 4 - 'Flipping the Negative'
(reframing the 'facts' to offer a positive interpretation)

Now, we are going to invite a thought to come to our attention and gentle focus. Where this thought is persisting in negativity, 'flip it'.

For example:

"I'll never get the hang of this meditation malarkey."

Flip it to:

"I'm already doing it right because I am noticing my thoughts and it reminds me that I am bigger than those thoughts."

EXERCISE 5 - 'Full spectrum thinking:
Hold on with Both Hands'
(using polarity to find perspective)

How we think and how we feel are often at odds. If we can learn to hold opposites or conflicting thoughts and feelings at the same time, we can resolve the paradox within ourselves.

Think about how all things have their opposite sides of the coin, opposing ends of a spectrum and that 'everything is because it isn't'. Cognitive dissonance - the experience of awkwardness that we have when two conflicting thoughts - creates a quandary over our values, decision making or ability to think clearly.

This technique is my own mental-emotional habit which formed when I was around 14 and struggling with an absence of having any literal religious faith. It also draws on both cognitive dissonance and Janusian Thinking (named by Albert Rothenburg after the god Janus who simultaneously looked to the past and the future).

This technique is all about holding space in time - for all possibilities, not just the one you are thinking of.

For example:

"This is a load of old cobbleballs and isn't working."

Also hold the opposite idea...

"This is a simple and astonishing way to experience reality."

Somewhere in the middle, you will likely settle until you nail this practice and see the results.

Holding opposing thoughts at same time - without judgement i.e. not choosing either state relates us back to quantum entanglement. Being able to hold both means you are creating all the possible choices.

Once you realise the benefit of being able to hold opposing thoughts or views simultaneously, the journey to Enlightenment really begins.

Ironically, this state of flux shows you not only two views, but a gap in the middle where neither view is held - and here in this gap we find ourselves falling down the rabbit hole of infinite potential.

So, think like Alice in Wonderland and let go of binary thinking. No black and White, no good or bad, no right or wrong. It's all whatever you make it.

Follow with...

EXERCISE 6 - *'Ask a different organ'*
(embodied emotion)

The body has a wisdom of its own and sometimes we tend to just assume that our entire conscious experience (or mind) belongs in the brain. 'Feeling' it up here in our heads where our eyes, ears, nose and mouths are all actively filtering information is understandable. It seems as though the brain is always the seat of 'truth' but if we consider that the brain is one of many organs in our holistic body (and is the organ who named itself and all the others) we can see why important information from other organs goes unnoticed.

Begin to pay attention to the sensations in your heart, solar plexus and stomach areas and notice the embodied positive emotion you are experiencing. Remember, if it feels like butterflies in your tummy, it is excitement for your new positive vision, if it feels like racing heart remember it is excitement for your new vision and so on. You can also 'dial down' the sensations anytime you wish.

Allow the excitement, love and joy to expand and grow INTO the time and space you have created. You can also 'dial up' the excitement if you feel you'd like to. This heightened sense of anticipation and positivity will of course, magnify the efficacy of your work.

Become fully and completed immersed, saturated with this feeling. The bigger and brighter the better. You are now FULLY FEELING this emotion as you hold the positive vision (or thoughts). You are now making this YOU the reality. When you feel you have the vision and the feeling so fully aligned or synched, smile and then thank yourself and the Universe for the will being done.

Congratulations! You are now that new YOU, on the road to that specific vision. You are manifesting your reality. You are turning your anxious skills into a powerhouse of Creation.

Important! Know that it has been done and that no doubt or worry nor anxious thought that might follow on can undo it. Manifesting only fully works when the full and complete intention is there to align (or synch) both vision and feeling. This is why although you can make yourself ill, unlucky and unhappy by persistent negativity over time, you cannot accidentally manifest something terrible that just pops up in your head. Those pop-up thoughts or feelings are not the same as the intentional work you have done.

Now follow with...

The DOING bit...

EXERCISE 7 - 'Trust your counter-intuition'

Notice any gut feelings you have about what to do next. If you are noticing a pull to do something and that naysayer is telling you to distract yourself with something else, like self-criticism or pairing socks, then remember - trust that your counter intuition is an echo of your Anxiety instinct telling you to stay safe, trying to keep your from taking a risk.

Thank it for drawing it to your attention and reminding you to listen to your intuition. Use 'Flipping the negative' or Janusian Thinking here too, if that helps to quieten the worry.

EXERCISE 8 - *'Doubt and Do it anyway'*
(Positive Risk Taking)

It is time to take that new embodied you on your first physical 'real world' steps to manifesting the vision. Even if doubt is aboard the new ship YOU, that is totally OK. Remember doubts are those ironic reminders that you primarily have faith in yourself.

What are you going to do now? It might look like this:

- going for a walk and allow it all to percolate
- making a certain phone call or email
- reaching out to someone with expertise
- asking for help at home
- writing your plan
- beginning your research
- revisiting a source of inspiration
- telling someone you trust your new truth
- blogging

What comes to mind? Where will you go Now?

What do you now know, believe and have faith in - that you need to do next?

What positive risks are you about to take on your journey of personal development?

How does it feel to know that you are now going from Anxiety to Enlightenment?

CHAPTER FIVE

IN CONCLUSION, LET'S BEGIN...

All roads lead to where you started

Think back to the beginning of our IF adventure where I talked about being the hero(ine) of your own journey. So now we come full circle, by which I mean, of course *spiral*.

The hero's journey begins with an innocent person being 'called' to action, who then leaves their comfort zone of home, is tried and tested, meets and seeks and meets again others along the way, finds their own treasure - their personal enlightenment.

The treasure usually takes on a metaphorical form e.g. finding the 'holy grail' (the key to eternal life, and where we get the 'grail quest' idea from), or to 'rescue the innocent' (to stand for justice, liberty and honour), to save a princess (to find love) and so on. Only once the treasure is found, the hero returns home - but has changed forever. They have grown. They have in many ways come around to their starting point - but not in a simple frustrating loop but instead on an upward spiral because they have grown and expanded through overcoming their struggles, setbacks and fears.

This journey is each of our lives - we are born of star dust and we will return to it, but through the journey of our lives from birth to death (and beyond), we are the changed or transformed hero. The journey is the series of opportunities for risks, for change, for growth.

Perhaps you feel that you might still be at the beginning of your journey, yet to take those steps? Well, that's all good. This is your moment to hear the call.

In being called to action, we must first 'hear the call' and ironically, it may have been a repeating call you have heard all your life - you are just a master of ignoring it. Anxiety is great at helping you avoid taking action through distraction, procrastination and doubt.

The call comes around on the spiral because each time you hear it, the circumstances are different and you are different. The call can be anything - but you know or at least suspect it's your personal calling because it is a consistent yearning and you feel it pulling you forward and upward to a higher purpose.

It's time to choose what you will do next.

You can stay as you are or, you can move. Move in any direction, it doesn't really matter which, because your journey will flow and follow the spiral of growth.

Too many of us travel through life on a loop, going nowhere. What prevents us from answering our call to action, for setting out on our grail quest is not Anxiety itself but how we *experience* it. This is why IF seeks to reinterpret our physical sensations as excitement for possibility, to expand our thoughts to create unlimited potential and to understand our emotions as messages from our core values, our soul. Aligning these in the one coherent protagonist is exceptionally potent for adventure.

You see, as an anxious person, you are blessed with having amazing mental skills, a highly sensitive instrument that is your body, a powerhouse of emotionality and a heart that cares. The hero could not be better equipped!

Only through conscious will, our desire to move forward can we break the negative cycles of fear, low mood and stagnation and transmute the weight that holds us stuck into that golden force that pushes us forward. Here we take action - positive risk-taking that is aligned with our quest for personal Enlightenment.

What is keeping you back... that could be at your back?

There is a double irony to be found in our anxious stagnation. We become anxious at the idea of never growing in life, never finding meaning and purpose; never satisfying those 'Big Questions'. Yet the typical reasons underlying the avoidance of moving forward in life are our anxieties about the journey itself.

These are both literal and metaphorical:

- Fear of leaving home/comfort zone
- Fear of change or being different
- Fear of social exclusion and shame
- Fear of what you might find
- Danger or risk

What comes to your mind?

Be honest with yourself and notice it - its truth will set you free to roam.

When you are Lost you are Found

It's time now to really move forward so consider this...

If you cannot see the way ahead, you are not lost. You are simply undecided. This means you have choices.

You can choose anything.

If you keep finding yourself stuck in your life's progress, you may find yourself saying that you are 'without direction', 'at a crossroads' or just cannot see the way ahead. Consider this: maybe you are supposed to forge a new path?

Some of us feel a 'calling' - perhaps religious or spiritual or, scientific. They are the same calling. Whatever form it takes, the call is one to step forward on the quest before you.

Here, the further along you travel, you also have the opportunity for leadership. Now there is no need to feel alarmed - feel excited! Leadership is simply taking ownership of your journey and daring to grow step by step - despite the uncertainties. In fact, *because* of the uncertainties.

Others might simply love what you represent and choose to follow your direction - but they do so in their *own* footsteps. Children, friends, colleagues, social media followers and strangers - all of us seek others for inspiration and at times, a light in the dark. In turn we are each a beacon for someone else.

If you are feeling that 'calling' to forge a new path and/or to lead others - and the thought still terrifies you... then it's a sign that you are made of the right star stuff. You make choices as *considered, heart-felt* positive risks.

You *care.*

Your self-doubt assures you of your understanding that leadership is not simply being at the front, it is also a task. That if you were not anxious about leading, then either you simply already know the road - that it's tried and tested and therefore not your own, or, someone else is actually taking the steps for you.

True heart-centred leadership is only born of those who are willing to keep stepping ahead in spite of, and because of, their uncertainties. Ironically, it is in the presence of self-doubt that they can be assured of enough faith to move forward.

> *"Every great dream begins with a dreamer.*
> *Always remember, you have within you the strength,*
> *the patience, and the passion to reach for the stars*
> *to change the world."*
> **Harriet Tubman**

Think of it this way too, you can never heal if you are never injured. You can never be serene if you have never worried. You can never be 'found' if you were never lost. Pain, worry, feeling scared or lost are all forms of Anxiety and they are all perspectives held in a moment of experience. In a moment of potential change. Surrendering to the uncertain opens up all the potential for you.

It's what you *choose to do now* that will define your reality.

Stepping into the moment with faith in yourself is the only option for growth. Count your blessings, those double-sided coins and accept the paradoxical wealth in your purse, your ironic strengths and your heartfelt will to grow - with all your Anxiety has taught you, firmly at your back.

Where will you choose to go?

What direction will you take?

What is the next step?

What if you have all the choice in the universe?

What...if?

To find out more and gain further support on your journey, visit us at

www.ironicfundamentalism.com

Printed in Poland
by Amazon Fulfillment
Poland Sp. z o.o., Wrocław